To a wonderful friend Eleanor

MY WAR

by Bob Swirsky

ISBN 978-0-615-42087-5

Printed in the United States of America

My War

Dedication:

<u>My War</u> is dedicated to Molly Levine Swirsky, who has been my steadfast partner for 64 years, and to my children and grandchildren, to whom I leave my legacy. Without the support and help of my wife in the anguished years of my post war recovery, I would not be here to tell this story, and without the inspiration of my children, Debby and Tom, Mindy, and Michael, and my grandchildren, Ben, Jenna, and Michael, my resolve to pass on the lessons of <u>My War</u> would have lacked its mooring.

I also want to dedicate this book as a tribute to the courageous men and women of the Third Armored Division, and to the countless lives - military and civilian - that were sacrificed in our battle for freedom.

Prologue:

My War is the story of only one man, myself, Tech Sergeant Bob Swirsky, among millions of men and women who participated in World War II. I was one of many who was fortunate to come back alive, perhaps not sound of mind for several years, but sound of body. It is a story which involves, whether noted or not in the book, all branches of the service, and which honors all those who paid the ultimate price. My experiences were obviously shared by 14 million brave men and women serving in the U.S. Armed Forces on many fronts, including air, land, and sea. There were many heroes who gave their lives for freedom.

My War is being written in the years 2009 and 2010. It is not just a book of memoirs, but relates personal experiences woven into the combat sequences. It is a tale, not only of the horrors of war, but also of some of the lighter moments that my crew and I experienced throughout 323 days of actual combat as part of the 486th Anti Aircraft Artillery (Automatic Weapons) Self Propelled Battalion, attached to the 3rd Armored Division, First Army.

World War II movies and books by this time are "old hat," but they have sparked the interest of a new generation, including average citizens and elementary school, high school, and college students who have become World War II buffs. I hope the following story will enlighten them.

I shall begin…

Where I Came From:

I was born in Bridgeport, Connecticut on November 22, 1919. World War I had ended on November 11th, 1918. Prior to its ending, my father was hit by the flu epidemic of the times. He also received his draft notice at the same time. Because of his severe illness, his entry into the U.S. Army was put on hold. My mother nursed him back to health, and on the morning of November 11th, he was on his way to the train station planning to travel to the induction center. As he was about to board the train with a group of other inductees, the factory whistles in the entire industrial city of Bridgeport, Connecticut sounded. This signified that World War I had ended. Consequently, my father never boarded that train. Instead, he was sent home and never had to serve in the U.S. Army. Years later, in January of 1943, I would board a train at the very same station to be inducted into the army.

A Recollection:

I was about 10 years old and had a friend who lived around the corner whose father collected books on World War I. My friend and I would look through them wide-eyed. The pictures were of dead soldiers, emaciated civilian bodies, carcasses of horses and cows, severely destroyed cities, and battlefields and trenches. Little did I realize then that many years later, I would see the same type of horror when I served in the U.S. Army as part of the 3rd Armored Division. That would come when I was in my early twenties.

Now, at the age of 90, I am writing my memoirs in book form

entitled <u>My War</u> so that my children and grandchildren will understand their father's/grandfather's role and some of his personal experiences in World War II.

The following stories may not all be in exact sequence, and each chapter, in itself, could be elaborated into a book; however, I hope that my personal story will enhance the reader's understanding of what he/she has learned through history books about World War II and that he/she will take away with him/her a life lesson.

Beginning of it All -
Pearl Harbor Day - December 7th, 1941:

It was a quiet afternoon, somewhere around 1 p.m. Two friends of mine, Frank ("Lefty") Fasanella and Nick DiNapoli, and I were sitting in my house, listening to the radio. Glen Miller's "Chattanooga Choo Choo" was playing on the radio when the program was interrupted by the announcement that Pearl Harbor had been bombed by the Japanese. Shortly after, President Roosevelt, in one of his first famous fireside speeches, declared it a day of infamy and said that we were now at war with Japan. The three of us were eager to become part of the U.S. Army and do our share in combating our new enemy. Eventually, Nick went into the Marines and fought in the islands of the Pacific. "Lefty," having been examined and found to have an ear problem, would not have to serve.

My Status and How it Changed:

After I received my draft card, I was offered a job in a munitions factory by one of the head men at the factory who knew me personally. I turned it down because I wished to go into the service and did not want to be deferred. However, after receiving my physical, I was labeled a 4F because the examining physician told me that I had a very high blood pressure. I really wanted to serve, and it hurt to be told that I was going to be knocked off. Knowing how much I wanted to be a part of the armed forces, my brother insisted that I go to his doctor to have a physical. This doctor confirmed that I had a fluctuating blood pressure but said that it would not affect army duty, as I was perfectly healthy otherwise. A few months later, I was called by the Draft Board for re-examination. After passing all parts of the examination, the doctor said my blood pressure was high, and I was out. I told him what had happened the first time and how my personal doctor had explained the definition of a fluctuating blood pressure to me. He would not prescribe medication because there was nothing wrong with me. I asked the army doctor to allow me to sit for 15 minutes and then to come back and take my blood pressure again. He did just that, and when he came back and retook my pressure, it was normal. I was very happy, and the doctor's comment was, "Okay, bud, it's your funeral." I thanked him, and I now visualized myself in the uniform of a U.S. soldier.

A Day to Remember - Train to Fort Devens in Ayers, Massachusetts:

I received notice from the local Draft Board that I was to report to the Bridgeport Railroad Station on January 10th at 5 a.m. to board a train which was to take me and others to Fort Devens in Massachusetts. In my father's old International truck, he and I arrived at the station at about 4:30 a.m. As we had half an hour until the train was scheduled to arrive, we went to a little enclosed stand underneath the railroad station and had a cup of coffee together while we waited for 5 o'clock. The thirty minutes flew by.

When it was time to depart, my father wanted to go to the platform with me, but I told him not to do it because I felt that it would be too hard on both of us to have to say goodbye. With tears in his eyes, he reluctantly went back to his truck. I could see that he waited in the street until the train arrived and I boarded it with about 27 inductees from Fairfield County. One of the inductees was a baker who worked for a local bakery named Zouderers in Bridgeport, and he had made a large chocolate layer cake. Once on the train, he gave each of the inductees a piece.

The ride to Fort Devens was rather a quiet one. I imagine that everybody, like myself, was wondering what the future would hold when we reached our destination. My thoughts were of what I was leaving behind - my friends, my family, and a lifestyle. Things would change dramatically, and there would be no more hanging out and having a beer with the guys, going bowling, taking a female friend to the amusement park at Pleasure Beach, watching Fox Movie-tone news depicting war scenes, or movies at the Palace and Majestic Theaters. As the train drew closer to its destination, my daydreaming came to an end, and there was now an unknown future to be faced. I wondered whether I would ever return.

Arrival at Fort Devens on January 10th, 1943:

Upon arriving at Fort Devens, those of us who were on the train from the Fairfield County area were put into barracks with men from other areas. I now realized that my army life had begun. The odors of food cooking in a mess hall and the smell of wood stoves permeated the air. Once we were somewhat settled in the barracks, we received our first taste of army food. It consisted of hot cereal, scrambled eggs, and a glass of milk. I must have been very hungry because it tasted like a gourmet meal. During our three day stay at the fort, a few men who raised their hands when volunteers were asked for while in formation found out that they were going to be on "KP" and learned that it meant "kitchen duty." This taught us never to raise our hands when a sergeant asked for volunteers. One either wound up becoming a latrine specialist, cleaning toilet bowls and floors, or an expert in serving food, washing dishes, and peeling potatoes!

Shortly thereafter, we were marched in a rather ragged formation, scantily clad in rain coats, to receive shots in one building. A very strong fellow from Maine actually fainted when the needle penetrated his arm. Then we were sent to other buildings to listen to orientations on what to expect of the army, rules of behavior, and a lecture on the hygiene of our bodies. At that point, we had to wait for further orders.

During the few days together, friendships were made, some only lasting a short time, as we soon would be split up. Speculating among us began, and some thought we might head for California where the weather would be nice and warm. If we wound up in California, my assumption was that we would end up in the Pacific fighting the Japanese.

On approximately the third day, many of our names were called, and we were to gather our belongings and fall out outside of the barracks. We were marched on a cold and misty morning to an assembly area to await a train, and we did not know in which direction that train would be going. Once on board, we learned that the train was heading south, and then all were sure that we would be going to Europe to fight the Axis.

After a long ride, we reached our destination, Camp Davis,

North Carolina. The camp was situated near a small town called Holly Ridge. For the most part, the men from Fairfield County who had boarded the train in Bridgeport, Connecticut were kept together. Now, although those of us who had become friends might be separated into different batteries of the 486th AAA (AW) SP Battalion, we would remain friends throughout the entire training program and eventually the war in Europe. Of course, some did not return because they gave their lives for their country.

Arrival at Camp Davis and What Followed:

Approximately 500 of us arrived at the camp on January 16th, 1943. Our basic training grounds were to be at Camp Davis for several months to come. We were taken by trucks to a group of long, wooden barracks, which would be our living quarters while at Camp Davis. The place must have been built on swamp land because it was muddy and there were ditches which were apparently there to drain off water in front of the barracks. After we settled in, I and a fellow soldier named Emil Troll, who was from Trumbull, Connecticut, found ourselves digging a ditch in front of our barracks a little deeper than it already was. It probably was not necessary to dig the ditch deeper; however, it gave us a preview of what was to come, as there would be many foxholes and slit trenches to be dug in the future.

Although the next day was Sunday, our scheduled routine began at the early hour of 5 a.m. From then on, we were con-stantly on the go in weather that was raw and cold.

Very shortly after arrival, we were given Tetanus shots. Our arms hurt so much from the shots that we could hardly lift them, and we would help each other put on our shirts and outerwear. Also, we were issued our uniforms, and many were given M1s and appropriate guns. A few days later, another 250 men arrived at the camp. They looked at us in awe, not knowing that we had been there only a few days before them. We told them what to do, and they practically jumped, as they did not realize that we had no actual authority and were just doing what the Cadre had told us to do. Cadre were soldiers who had already experienced enough army life to be able to instruct new arrivals. They acted tough and hard and tried to bear down on us. Some of the new arrivals were intimidated, but some of the inductees were just as tough as the Cadre and took the Cadre down a peg. One soldier who was really given the works (and in those days, one did not write home to mother for sympathy) took matters into his own hands by going behind the barracks with the Cadre, and the Cadre came out with the worst of it. I believe it helped all the new inductees because consequently, we were all treated more humanely.

The main instructors in our Cadre consisted of Corporal Guertz, Sergeant Moody, Sergeant Gilmore, and Sergeant Tims. Corporal Guertz tried to impress us with his toughness and reminded me of the movie actor James Cagney. Sergeant Moody was quiet and not the rugged type. He treated the inductees with a lot of compassion. Sergeant Gilmore was a heavyset man, who lacked authority as far as the men were concerned. Sergeant Tims had spent 7 years in the Merchant Marine and had sailed the seven seas before entering the army. He was a heavy drinker and would come in at 1 a.m., half loaded, wake everyone, and give them orders to scrub the floors. In spite of his drinking, we had to follow his orders because he had rank. However, when he was sober, he was a great guy and someone to whom you could tell your troubles.

It was not too long before we were finally a full battalion of about 900 men. The battalion consisted of four batteries - A,

B, C, and D – and Headquarters. The complete outfit was now the 486th AAA (AW) SP Battalion. After we were all assigned our places, I was part of C Battery. Among our new friends were men who had come from as far west as California. Some came from as far north as Caribou, Maine; others came from Kentucky, Indiana, and many other states too. Basically, though, we were largely a New England group, with a great many of us coming from Maine, Massachusetts, and Connecticut.

After settling into camp life and training, one of our routines at the end of a day would be to go the "PX" and gorge ourselves on Clark Bars and Cokes. On weekends, if we obtained passes, we were allowed to go into Holly Ridge, the small town on the outskirts of camp. Holly Ridge was reminiscent of an old western movie town with a saloon and a general store where people could purchase their wares. One of the store front windows displayed embroidered pillows which said "Love you, Mom" or a message meant for wives or girlfriends. These were mementos intended to be sent home to reassure family/loved ones that all was well. I often wondered why there was never a message for "Dad." There was also a beer joint which we often visited, but it eventually became off limits to us due to some inebriated men in our outfit who created a brawl a la western style.

It was not long before we were called, one at a time, into a Day Room (a place where we could relax, write letters, listen to a piano player, and do as we wished) to receive GI haircuts by Louie Ferrigno (who had been a barber in Norwalk, Connecticut). Some of the men were very upset, as no one was asked how they wanted their hair to be cut. All haircuts were exactly the same. When my turn came, Louie asked, "Do you realize that you are almost bald on top?" Although it bothered me then, now, at the age of 90, I pay no mind to the spot that still shows up as very sparse.

Speaking of the Day Room and the opportunity to write letters home, there was a boy from Maine who always asked me to help him spell words, so consequently I was able to see what he was writing. As he had raised chickens back home, it always amused me that, when writing to his wife, his letters would always begin with the words "Mary, how are the chickens?" I felt bad for his wife, as it seemed that he was more concerned about the chickens than Mary!

Now, with our new haircuts and our uniforms and guns having been issued, we looked the part of awkward, yet proud, newly indoctrinated soldiers. We were ready to go into an intensive physical training program which put some of us into the camp's hospital wards with colds and fevers. If anyone showed a temperature of 100 degrees or more, they were hospitalized. Louie Bianci, from Trumbull, Connecticut, and I once shared a room in the hospital ward, and we drove the nurses crazy. Each of the three nights that we were there, as we both loved chocolate milk, we drank most of it from the refrigerator in the hall near our room and ate some of the food. Each morning, the nurse would reprimand us in a good natured way. A few weeks later, I re-entered the hospital for one day with severe pains in my head, which was attributed to a sinus infection. My sinuses were drained, and I returned to duty the same day.

Camp Davis Training:

Our day started at 5 a.m. when we were awakened with Reveille. We were given about ten minutes to get out of the barracks and line up in formation on the pavement, ready to run approximately ¼ of a mile around a camp block. If someone was not fully clothed, he ran as he was. This exercise showed that most of the guys were not in the best physical shape, as they actually limped back into the camp huffing and puffing. Upon returning, we had a few minutes to take a deep breath and go to the mess hall for breakfast. Usually, the meal was so good that some men would say they actually had found a home in the army. After breakfast, we would wash our mess gear in a can full of steaming hot water, then rinse it in another can. Next, we had to get back to the barracks to make sure our bunks were made properly, and then the day was to start with IDR (infantry drill) under the bark of Corporal Guertz.

I was always one of the last persons in everything being/getting done because my last name initial was "S," putting me near the end of every line. Consequently, I always felt pressured to keep up with the rest.

Our physical training was so intense that the label given to the entire battalion was "Every man a commando." After breakfast and inspection were over, our daily physical regimen began with 30 obstacles through which we had to run. This was done wearing full gear, which included helmet, cartridge belt, full canteen, and a loaded backpack. (We did not have to carry our bayonets and our rifles for the course.) The pack, which was meant to carry approximately 60 pounds, weighed almost half as much as I did.

Among the 30 obstacles which we were required to overcome were scaling a 10 foot wall, going up a 30 foot rope hand over hand to a small platform and coming down the other side on a ladder-type rope, and hurdling an 8 foot ditch which had water in it.

The last obstacle was the easiest. It was the parallel bars. However, if one walked from the bars to the finish line, which was about 25 feet away, one had to repeat the entire course again, as the whole course was to be done on the run.

Next, we were given a five minute break so that if one wished to relax or have a cigarette, he could do so. Then came the push ups. We were required to do 50 push ups without our stomachs falling in. Then, we were given another five minute break, and after this break, we had to pick someone our size or a bit heavier, and we were trained in the art of Jiu Jitzu. Still, after another break, came a 5 mile run on a hot dirt road. (Eventually, to see how we had progressed in our physical training, for a day, the run was increased to 10 miles on a heavily traveled, hot tarred city road on a 92 degree day, and every man finished strong.) On our hikes, we were stimulated by singing as we marched along led by Paul Sverni, who gave us the cue, e.g., on those ballad verses which ended with the words "Gee, but I want to go home." Incidentally, one did not fall out on these marches without some sort of punishment. One of our boys constantly complained about his back, so he was given the cure - digging a ditch - and that stopped the complaint.

At this point, we had learned a lot about our individual guns, which included the M1 rifle and the 50 caliber and 30 caliber machine guns, and how to use them at a firing range. I got a kick out of firing the 50 caliber machine gun at a target which would be an improvised tank moving across a track.

Another part of the training was called an infiltration course. We were required to crawl on our stomachs on a stretch of dirt under barbed wire while small explosions went off unexpectedly around us and while live machine guns were firing over our heads. We had to keep our heads down, as close to the ground as possible; otherwise, we could have been severely injured or killed. Rumor had it that three soldiers in a battalion in Texas had been hit.

Then there were bivouacs where, for a day and a night, we learned how to "rough it" in wooded areas in order to prepare

for the circumstances of actual combat. We would sleep out-
doors on bedrolls in tents, make fires over which to cook our
meals, and dig slit trenches in order to "relieve" ourselves.

There was a time when we trudged through a muddy swamp
over downed tree branches in water sometimes up to our knees
for a period of close to 6 hours. One battery went 15 miles off
course because the sergeants in charge did not read their com-
passes properly. A truck had to be sent out to bring them into
camp just in time for supper.

Another time on a Friday evening, after all our gear had been
cleaned, our clothing put in order on our shelves, our shoes pol-
ished, and everything made ready for the usual Saturday morning inspection, we were awakened at 1 a.m. and taken through
a rain storm on a 16 mile hike. During the hike, one of the soldiers, who eventually was given a Section 8, kept raising his
voice when he shouldn't have opened his mouth. When the hike
was completed and we arrived back at the camp, we had just
enough time to dry out and be ready for the Saturday morning
inspection. As I was entitled to a weekend pass, I went to the
Charge of Quarters to pick it up, and the First Sergeant who
was there at the time told me that the lieutenant who had accompanied us on the hike had "gigged" me for my actions on
the hike and my pass was rescinded. It seems that he had con-
fused my last name with another soldier's last name - the one
who I mentioned had received a Section 8 before we went overseas - because both names ended in "sky." When my battery
commander learned of the error, he offered me a 3 day pass to
Wilmington. Not wishing to go alone, I turned it down.

Another day involved a 28 mile hike. That particular day, I had
already been going to radio school, so I was freed of it.

Evenings involved orientation on all our weapons, aircraft identification, radio procedures, and what to expect someday in

combat, and we underwent questioning to see what we had learned and understood. Although we did not have radios in our tracks, we were briefed and told what to expect once we were given them. An emphasis was placed on accuracy, as communication among all elements of our units would be of the utmost importance.

Relaxation in the evenings would come after all the orientation classes were over. I spent many restful moments in the Day Room listening to a fellow soldier who was a piano player by the name of Walt Le Seur. Walt reminded me of the movie celebrity Fred MacMurray (well known for playing the father, Steven Douglas, in the television show "My Three Sons"). Walt was very much like him physically and facially. His favorite song, which became my request wherever I went, was "Sunny Side of the Street." Everyone loved Walt because of his happy-go-lucky personality, and he kept us all in good spirits with his piano playing. During training in Camp Davis, one of our men, Milton Cohen, who was a musician in his own right, assembled a band, and we were the lucky recipients of many concerts.

When going back to the barracks from the Day Room at 11 p.m., we would hear "Taps," which, to this day, brings tears to my eyes. Our living quarters were usually cold, and we had a pot belly stove to keep ourselves somewhat warm. Each night some of us would gather around the stove, and one of our buddies from Bridgeport, Connecticut by the name of Hamilton ("Mac") McQueen would sing a short song. All I can remember was that it ended with the words "down by the river." Then, when everyone was settled into their bunks, Charles Gassett from Maine would start telling jokes, and we would fall asleep laughing. These performances by McQueen and Gassett were of great importance, as they gave all the men a lift in spirits. Believe it or not, as tough as some of the men were, they would cry in their bunks at night, as they missed home and because of the intense training.

On those occasions when I received a weekend pass to Wilmington, North Carolina, I chose either to go to the beach, spend time writing letters at the USO, or see a movie. Prior to the movie starting and the curtains parting, music played. It always seemed to be the same song - Harry James playing and Helen Forrest singing - "It Seems to Me I Heard That Song Before." That song, to this day, along with "Sunny Side of the Street," remains something that takes me back to World War II.

On one of my two day passes to Wilmington, my buddies and I lost track of another buddy, George Abrams, and we could not find him. The day went by, and we found a church, which, in its basement, had mats placed on the floor for soldiers who would come looking for a place to sleep for the evening. We slept alongside of a piano. When morning came, we stood up and looked about, and there was George, asleep on top of the piano!

I would like to add an incidental tale of two soldiers' short-lived association with my battery. These two soldiers went about doing everything they could in order to get out of the outfit, or perhaps, even out of the army. One of them, who I will call "Private A," went as far as our last training camp, Camp Hulen, and the other, who I will call "Private B," never went with us beyond Camp Davis.

Private A would disrupt all aspects of basic training with unacceptable behavior. The consequence for his actions was that he was kept on base and given latrine duty everyday starting after breakfast while everyone else was going through the daily training. Although this detail was not a pleasant one, he made it into a good deal financially for himself. Latrine detail involved cleaning all the toilets, wash basins, and the floor, and he had to remain there all day. Talk was circulated amongst the guys that he would take in fatigues and wash and dry them for 75 cents a piece. In other words, he was not only cleaning the latrines, but was also raking in the bucks. Private A never did go overseas with us, but instead was given a "Section 8" discharge before we left the States. His last misdemeanor, which prompted the decision to leave him behind, had to do with the following. We were all required to have final physicals at Camp Hulen, which included having our teeth examined prior to being cleared for overseas duty. When the dentist, Captain Husky, approached Private A and asked him to open his mouth, Private A would scream "bloody murder." His screams could be heard throughout the area, and that sealed his fate. One of the fellows in our outfit kept in touch with him through letter writing and later told us that Private A had become an extremely wealthy and successful real estate man in his hometown of Chicago.

Private B was a pleasant, quiet, well-mannered young man. His tactics were entirely different than those of Private A. When we fell out in formation, he would never wear the proper dress. He would mix training clothes with dress clothes. It seemed he never did anything correct and made it look like it was not intentional. It was as if he was just not cut out to be a soldier. He also had one bad habit. He would not shower or wash. As a result, the guys in his barracks would drag him into the shower room, strip him, and scrub him with a brush until he actually bled. Due to his improper hygiene, Private B was not allowed to eat in the mess hall with the others. He could fill his mess kit, and then he had to sit on the deck entrance to the mess hall. Usually, the consequence for his actions was never more severe than kitchen duty. However, because of his behavior, he was transferred to the base hospital. A week later, he paid us a visit. He was handsome in his uniform, clean shaven, and beaming from ear to ear. He was invited to eat with us in the mess hall during this visit and related to us the details of what he was now doing. He told us that he was very happy. As I saw it, he had wanted out of a combat battalion and had gotten his wish. After that one visit, we had no more contact with him.

How I Acquired the Job of Radio Operator:

A notice had been put on the bulletin board that there would be a position in the battery for a radio operator. This would involve undergoing several weeks of training. I put my name on the board with two other names, and I was chosen. The schooling was on base within a few miles' walking distance of the area where my barracks were located. While I attended school, the physical part of the outfit's training was going on. Therefore I was separated from the rough stuff that the rest of the men were going through. I was on a totally different schedule, and different meant that I didn't have to answer to anyone.

During the week, school began at 9 a.m. and ended at 3 p.m., and there was no school on the weekends. During the school day, instruction included intense Morse Code and radio operations training. We also learned how to use hand generators.

Once the radio schooling was over, I was expected to join the others in the physical part of the training, which was similar to commando training. In addition, I attended night orientation classes on aircraft identification, guns, and other related subjects. I also had to give talks and answer questions on radio procedures.

On the first day of a 5 mile run, while the others did not even break a sweat, I could not keep up and fell out of the line. Corporal Milton Cohen, from Bridgeport, Connecticut, pushed me back in line, telling me not to quit and that I must continue because otherwise there could be consequences such as digging a 6' by 6' garbage pit. I fell back into the run, got my second wind, and from then on, it was a breeze. Going over a 10 foot fence and up a 30 foot rope, hand over hand, and going through many more challenging obstacles soon became easy to accomplish.

Once again, speaking about radio schooling, I was not the fastest code operator, but more importantly, I was accurate, and in combat, accuracy would prove to be more important. As far as voice radio was concerned, I was rated Number 1.

Later on, Louisiana Maneuvers would give me simulated combat experience. However, the actual combat experience, where lives would be at stake, would soon come on the European continent.

Radio Operation:

Being a radio operator sometimes necessitated that I have weekend duty. This job required me to operate a switchboard in our battalion radio center that was hooked up to the main camp radio station which could receive messages from the city of Wilmington, North Carolina. I would be there from 5 p.m. until 5 a.m. - 12 hour duty. There was no Morse Code. It was strictly voice.

One weekend when I was on duty, somewhere around 11 p.m., the switchboard alerted me to an incoming call. It was coming from Wilmington, North Carolina to the Camp Davis communications center regarding a major car accident involving soldiers from our base. They were not, however, from my battalion. The operator at the Camp Davis communications center who had made the initial call from Wilmington had long conversations with me intermittently when she was not on another line. We spoke until I went off duty at 5 a.m. Before I went off duty, we learned more about each other, and I asked her if I might see her that evening. She said that would be okay, and I was to meet her where she was stationed, which was a large building which housed the main communication system for the camp. While I waited for her, a woman approached me and told me that the young lady would be down shortly. I sat there wondering what she would look like. As she was coming down the staircase from the second floor, I looked up and was not disappointed. As I always seemed to compare look-a-likes in people, she could have been a second Francis Langford, the movie actress. We had a pleasant evening. She had a curfew, and I never saw her again, as army duties prevented this.

Furlough Home:

Now that our basic training was over, we marched in full uniform on the Camp Davis parade grounds before a general and his aides. There were many other soldiers from different units in the camp who also participated in the review before the various commanding officers. Once the ceremonies were over, our battalion, all 900 of us, was pulled aside to stand on bleachers. All of the officers of our battalion sat in front, and a picture was taken.

Our next move would be to leave Camp Davis to go into the woods of Louisiana to take part in maneuvers. Since there was to be an interval of a few weeks before our move to Louisiana, a few of us were given furloughs. I was one of those chosen. I looked forward to seeing my family and friends. Heading home, I had to switch trains in Fayetteville, North Carolina. I had been standing on the platform too close to the rails, and the approaching train came in so silently that I did not hear it. It brushed my suitcase and nudged my shoulder. I was fortunate that it was traveling at a very slow speed; otherwise, I might have been injured. The train ride going home was so different than the one four months earlier heading for Camp Davis. It was an old train with straw seats, and I dozed practically all the way to New York City, where I had to switch trains for Bridgeport, Connecticut.

On arrival home, I was treated very warmly by all. My buddy "Lefty" Fasanella proved to be my chauffeur for the entire week I was at home. His father treated me like a son and insisted that I have my first meal with him and Mrs. Fasanella. My folks said that it was okay with them. Mr. Fasanella filled up his cocktail shaker, and I accompanied him to all his friends' houses to let them know that I was home, as they all knew me, having shared many a Christmas and New Year's Eve with them. When we returned to their home, Mrs. Fasanella had prepared a dinner of spaghetti and meatballs, which she knew was my favorite meal.

During the week, "Lefty" and I double-dated with the same girls that we had seen before the war. (When I came home at the end of the war, I discovered that these girls had married while I was away.) The week flew by, and I found myself boarding a train on the same platform where several months earlier I had been heading for Fort Devens. Instead, I was now traveling south to North Carolina.

My next mission before heading into the Louisiana maneuvers was to bring my half-track and others from the first and second platoons into Camp Polk to have radios installed. My track, in addition to two voice sets, was equipped with a Morse Code setup. It was given the call letters "3-Baker," which would remain through maneuvers and until the end of the war. Now we were prepared to go into maneuvers. They were conducted in vast woods in the areas of Leesville and Shreveport, and we engaged in these maneuvers with other units. There were mosquitoes that were like bombers and which were so plentiful that we slept underneath netting much of the time. The temperature was blistering hot, accompanied by torrential rainstorms. There were night convoys which could be very disturbing since the roads became covered with toads in the evenings. One could hear the crunching as the vehicles drove over them, and we could not change our course because of the toads. Incidentally, during maneuvers, as the Air Corps apparently needed men, we were asked whether anyone would like a transfer to the Air Corps. The only requirement would be to take another physical, which would place an emphasis on our eyesight. No one accepted the offer.

When we were issued passes to Leesville and Shreveport, we went shabbily dressed, as we had to take our uniforms out of barrack bags, and there was no way to press them. Hamilton McQueen and I slept in a flee-ridden hotel with shrieks going on throughout the night, and we slept through it all.

On one convoy over a very dusty road, we came into an area for inspection. Immediately after we pulled in, a high ranking officer, not of my battalion, but evidently a referee who rated the soldiers and outfits in maneuvers, and his aide mounted my track. One of the inspecting officers ran his fingers across our 50 caliber machine gun in the turret. He looked me in the eye and said, "Sergeant, your guns are dirty." I did not realize what I replied until I had actually said it. I answered the officer, "Sir, if you had come off dirt roads as we have done just now, your guns would be dirty. We just haven't had any time yet to clean our guns." (I probably should have used the word "anyone" instead of "you"; however, the words just slipped out of my mouth, and there was no taking them back.) Hearing my response, two of our officers who had accompanied the inspectors seemed shocked. I actually think that I saw them waiver back and forth, as they most likely felt like they would faint. However, I felt that the inspecting officers probably gave me credit for having the guts to respond as I had with the truth. After the inspection was over, I felt relieved because he had accepted my explanation and just told me to carry on.

As I recall, the maneuvers in Louisiana were conducted with elements of the 11th Armored Division. Restrictions were such that we were not allowed to go to a farm house and accept anything to eat, as we were supposed to be under combat conditions. However, in that neck of the woods, watermelons were delicious, and we were able to acquire them for 25 cents a piece from the people in the area unbeknownst to our officers.

During the maneuvers, a directive came down from higher up that we were going to a new destination. Our vehicles were dirty and needed cleaning, so we took them to the Sabine River and washed them. Instead of proceeding on, we were told that because of transportation difficulties on the roads to our next destination, we would return to Leesville for a short spell. It was about the 4th day of September when we headed for Camp Hulen, Texas.

Camp Hulen, Texas:

The route of march to Camp Hulen would take us through Texarcana, Austin, Beaumont, and Corpus Christie toward the Bay area, where eventually, the M15s and the M16s would spend ten weeks practicing firing at sleeves of slow moving aircraft. My vehicle, 3-Baker, would accompany them to the Bay so that if there was any communication to be had between the Bay and camp or between myself and the aircraft, it would be available. Meanwhile, we still had night classes and orientation that concentrated on aircraft identification and radio procedures.

When we had no other duties, we were given passes to Palacios, Texas, which was several miles from our base. Palacios was so small a town that one could walk from one end to the other in a very short amount of time. One trip to Palacios for me was very embarrassing. I met a young lady and invited her for a drink in a place called the Round House. It was given this name, as it was built in the shape of a circle. When we ordered drinks, the waitress refused to serve me. She said that I was too young and that I had to be 21 years of age. Fortunately, I was bailed out by my first sergeant, who saw my predicament and verified my age. When we had a full weekend, many of the men would go to the big city of Houston, Texas and stay at the Rice Hotel.

On one occasion, which happened to fall on the Jewish holiday of Rosh Hashana, our vehicles went to the bay to practice firing. Although I, and one other man, Edward Cohen, were of the Jewish faith, we were denied passes to observe the holiday by a lieutenant at Headquarters battalion, and we went with the others to the firing range. My battery commander, Captain De-Franco, saw Ed and me on our tracks. He angrily asked "What the hell are you guys doing here?" (The captain never swore, so for him to use the word "hell" showed how truly outraged he was that we had been denied passes on one of our most holy holidays. As a matter of fact, in basic training, if anyone was overheard using a swear word(s), he had to deposit a nickel in a box located in the Charge of Quarters office.) We told him that we had been denied passes by Headquarters, and he said, "I am getting you out of here!" Then he told his jeep driver Anctil to take us back to our base where we got dressed and were driven to a town called Rosenberg, which was named after a man who had a chain of food stores. After we attended services at a synagogue, a local family invited us to their home, and we had a wonderful dinner. Shortly thereafter, we headed back to the base.

While at Camp Hulen, some of us stayed in individual small gas heated houses which bunked about four people. In the middle of September, we were hit by heavy winds and rains, and much of the camp became inundated with water. Many of the small houses filled with water up to the bunks so that it was impossible to sleep there. Most of the battalion was evacuated to temporary quarters at Wharton's Fairgrounds. The storm became so intense that it bordered on being a hurricane. I, with my track, was put on a windswept corner in Wharton, Texas so that I could communicate via Morse Code with other cities or communicate by radio with Camp Hulen. There was a little store opposite our track on the corner which stayed open all night and kept my driver and me supplied with coffee so that we could stay awake (as if we would be able to sleep without the coffee during such circumstances!). When the storm abated, we returned to camp and resumed our normal functions.

Entertainment at Camp Hulen might be a show or a dance or a boxing match, which were all held at the local USO. One of the major boxing matches was between Cono DeSarli, who was the middleweight champion of our battalion, and the heavyweight champion of another outfit. It was to be strictly a six round exhibition bout. There was a big difference in the men's weight, one being a middleweight, and one being a heavyweight, and also in their height. At about the third round, the heavyweight boxer, putting aside the fact that it was an exhibition bout, clobbered Cono. Although a middleweight, Cono had a strong punch, probably as hard as a heavyweight could deliver. Cono angrily landed the heavyweight a vicious blow, and the heavyweight went down and was out cold for a good ten minutes. The wife of the heavyweight was so upset that she tried to attack Cono as he walked to his dressing room. Incidentally, when the war was over, Cono had boxed in 36 matches; 35 were wins, mostly knockouts, and the one which was not a win was a draw with a Golden Glove Champion of Chicago! (Cono eventually attained the title of Middleweight Champion of the 3rd Armored Division.)

Another member of the 486th boxing team, Paul Sverni, always bet money on Cono's fights. Cono would wink at Paul in between rounds when he felt that he might be able to knock out his opponent in the next round. Then, Paul, anticipating the insinuated outcome of the next round, would place a fast bet with someone in the one-minute intermission, coming out the winner nine out of ten times.

After 10 weeks of firing, which brought us to about the first week of October, the 486th Battalion AAA, (AW) SP, was deemed competent and ready to move on. However, it wasn't until about the second week of November that we packed our gear and left Camp Hulen. After we boarded a troop train, we were told by our officers that we were going to a place called Camp Shanks, New York and that this would be our last stop before being sent overseas to participate in the war in Europe. The train ride was an experience in itself. The sound of the train whistle as it traveled through various towns at night gave me an eerie feeling. I don't remember exactly the time that it took us to go across the country. However, I know that for two nights, we slept on the train, and during the days, we would stop in desolate areas so that we could get off the train and stretch our legs and do calisthenics. The trip was meant to be completely secret. We were not to engage in any conversation if a civilian approached us. At night, the window shades were drawn, and there was a guard stationed between each car to make sure that only the appropriate persons were on the train. Many of the men sang songs ("I Want to Buy a Paper Doll that I Can Call My Own" became a favorite) to pass the time away, and some played cards and/or held conversations about their personal lives.

Camp Shanks, New York:

Arriving at Camp Shanks, the battalion got down to very serious business. For the approximate week that we were there, each day we hiked and were involved in continual physical exercises, in addition to further orientation on various subjects, including classes on aircraft identification and radio procedures.

If we did not have any detail assigned to us, we were allowed to have a pass to leave camp for 12 hours, from 5 p.m. until 5 a.m. We were restricted and advised to go no more than 25 miles from camp, but New York City was considered to be just within the limit. I, and several of the men from Bridgeport, Connecticut, would take the bus from Camp Shanks to New York City, which left us off at 125th Street. As the train that went to Bridgeport from Grand Central Station stopped at 125th Street, we were able to be home from the City within an hour or so. On a couple of evenings, Ed Cohen and myself met his mother at the station at 125th station, and she drove us back to Bridgeport so that we did not have to take the train. Our evenings would be spent with families and friends, and then we would have to be back at the Bridgeport station to catch a 1 a.m. train back to 125th Street. There would be a bus waiting for us to take us back to camp. I had told my folks that the night I did not come home would mean that my stay in the States was over. Needless to say, I did not sleep much during that week, and when I got back after each visit at 5 a.m., I had to stand roll call. After breakfast, as we sat on our bunks, we listened once again to lectures. They were so boring that I almost fell asleep. One fellow actually did fall asleep and fell off of his bunk!

After lunch on the sixth day at Camp Shanks, we were watching a training film in the camp theater on how to administer medical treatment to a wounded soldier. The picture was gory, as it depicted a medic helping a soldier who had a stomach wound. At 3 p.m., the lights in the theater went on, and a speaker blurted out "All troops. Get back to your barracks, pack your belongings, and fall out on the street, and be ready to move out." We sat on our barrack bags for about 4 hours until evening, when we were told that we were leaving and to fall into a formation. We walked for about a half hour, lugging all our belongings to a train which was waiting to carry us further. The train let us off near a pier where a tremendous ship lay with its gang plank down, as if it was ready to be boarded. It was an awesome sight. The ship was painted battleship gray, and it was so long that one could not see either end of it in the darkness of night. We were told that we were about to board the Queen Mary, where there was heavy security evident. There were lights illuminating the pier around the gangplank, coffee was being given to the troops, and each individual unit was being called to start boarding. At the boarding plank was an M.P., and as I approached him when my name was called, he turned out to be a person with whom I had graduated from high school by the name of Seymour Kendall. We embraced, and he said to me, "I wish I was going with you."

Before we boarded the ship, each battery in our battalion had been notified where they were to go once on board. I was assigned as far down in the ship as one could possibly go. It was now 2 a.m., and I wound up sleeping on the bottom bunk of hammocks that were 5 tiers high. However, with all the movement going on, all I could do was to sit, cramped up, and wait until there was enough space around me where I could actually climb in and lay down. I slept in my clothes on the first night. Toward morning, many of us who could get up to the deck of the ship as it moved out from the pier and headed toward deeper water and the open ocean were able to see the Statue of Liberty. I was thrilled to see this sight, especially since we were leaving the country to preserve what she stood for.

Our 486th battalion men were given the responsibility of manning the anti-aircraft guns on the ship. This was to protect it from any enemy aircraft during its voyage across the ocean. I found out that the Queen Mary was probably transporting and setting a record number of people on this voyage of between 15,000 and 16,000 soldiers. Normally, during peace times, the ship would not carry more than 3,000 to 5,000 people.

I was given a detail on the ship to keep one of many staircases clean. I chose three men - DeSarli, DiNapoli, and Condon - who were from my battery to do the work. A lieutenant told me (I guess he had to show rank) that my crew had not done their job and to find them and have them sweep the staircase again. I went looking for them and found them in the ship's library, reading books. However, they were holding the books upside down, which of course meant that they were just pretending to read. I told them to keep doing what they were doing, as their detail could wait.

We had two meals a day. There were so many soldiers to be fed that when we lined up in the morning for breakfast, it seemed that we had never left the line because we were quickly back in line for the evening meal. We also had U.S.O. entertainment aboard the ship. I remember songs from Broadway shows being sung such as "People Will Say We're in Love" and "Evalina."

At one point while on board the Queen Mary, I felt a sudden surge of energy in the movement of the ship. It was explained later that a German submarine was on our tail and that we had outrun it. Because of the Queen's speed of 35 miles an hour, no other craft was capable of catching up with her. We arrived in Greenock, Scotland in less than six days. It was necessary for us to be taken off the ship to the dock on ferries, as the ship could not come in close enough to put down a gangplank.

We were greeted by musicians playing bagpipes and a bustling scene of people milling around the train which was waiting to take us to England. There were women in coveralls working feverishly with oil cans in their hands, oiling the wheels and getting the train ready to leave. Another sight we beheld was Clydesdale-type horses pulling wagons over cobblestone streets. It appeared as if they had kegs of beer loaded on them. To say the least, there was excitement in the air.

Once we were on the train, we were given coffee, doughnuts, and cigarettes by a group affiliated with the Red Cross. It wasn't long before we were on our way to our new destination in England. Songs were sung, and our favorite was "It's a Long Way to Tipperary." Soon it became quiet, and most of the men fell asleep as nightfall approached. Before the darkness fell, as I looked out of the windows, one of the things that struck me was the similarity of the rooftops of all the buildings, with the smoke stacks all forming the same pattern against the skyline.

As dawn arrived, we pulled into Semley Station in Wiltshire, England. Getting off the train, we had to cross over a small bridge to get to the army trucks which were waiting to take us to our new base. I was one of the last to leave the train. The sight was fitting for a movie scene. As the men crossed the bridge with the dawn breaking, the troops, with their barrack bags and guns, were silhouetted against the brightening sky. It was an awesome sight!

Life in England:

When we arrived in England, the 486th AAA (AW) SP Battalion, which was now officially attached to the 3rd Armored Division, was assigned to the First U.S. Army. We, the enlisted men, were brought to our quarters which were called "Quonset huts" on the property called Hays House. Because of the officers' ranks, their living quarters were in a mansion-type building. All of the battalion records were kept in this building, and that made it necessary for Headquarters personnel to sleep there in case the officers needed to refer to them. We spent our time hiking up and down hills and going through intense sessions, once again, on aircraft identification and radio procedures.

Now, as England was being heavily bombed at this point and was deeply involved in the war, and as the war in Europe had become crucial, the time had come for us to realize that we were an integral and actual fighting part of World War II. In one instance, 3-Baker and a couple of firing vehicles were put on a beach in Bournemouth, England. The purpose was to be on guard should German paratroopers try to land on English soil in the surrounding areas. We slept on the sand, and nearby, at the end of the beach, was a fish and chips concession. Frequently, we ate fish and chips wrapped in newspaper with our fingers. I have never since experienced anything as delicious in the U.S.

After an entire week on the beach, we returned to Hays House. On Friday nights, myself and two other men of the Jewish faith, Edward Cohen and Nate Laden of Bridgeport, Connecticut were invited for Sabbath suppers at a small house in East Noyle, which was approximately a mile from our quarters. The house was called the Bothy and was occupied by eleven land army girls, all of the Jewish faith, who worked in the fields for the English government. On the other side of the road from the

Bothy was another small house in which there was a stern mistress who supervised the girls and anybody who went in and out of the building. Although we were able to share time with the girls, there was a 10 p.m. curfew, at which time we had to leave. After a Friday night sabbath supper where the girls shared whatever food they had with us, one young lady, whose name was Goldina, would always give me a raw onion as I left because I loved onions. I would eat it on the way back to my quarters. One night I did not eat the onion, and it stayed in my pocket until the end of the war where it had become a piece of mush. After eating, we would retire to a small room where one girl played the guitar and all the other girls joined in and sang Israeli folk songs.

We practiced on and off landings from LCTs (landing crafts) with our M15s and M16s in the British Channel, and our firing vehicles also went to Camp Penhale in Cornwall for anti-aircraft firing. Back at the base, we still had our hikes up and down hills during the day, and continued classes on chemical warfare, combat intelligence, and radio operations. Emphasis was heavily placed on aircraft recognition, physical fitness, and radio procedures. My radio station, 3-Baker, was always involved in everything that went on.

For relaxation on weekends, we could get a pass to the town of Shaftesbury, where there was a U.S.O. building which served us 4 o'clock tea and refreshments. Sometimes there would also be entertainment there. At night, a pub was a pleasant place to relax, and where I normally would go to get that warm glass of Guinness Stout. They claimed Guinness Stout was good for pregnant women, but being that we men could not lay claim to being pregnant, that did not apply to us! I had many chats with the pub owners, and in particular, with an English gentlemen who was dressed in riding britches, looking as if he had just come from a fox hunt. He was always leaning on the bar, willing to accept an offer of a free beer.

Normandy:

When late May came, our battalion was moved out of Hays House to a concentrated area. We slept in a field for close to two weeks, waiting for orders to move to another area. On June 6, "D Day," as I lay on the ground, I heard the constant drone of aircraft over my head. I could not see where they were, but in my heart, I knew that the drone was so steady that something major was happening. It had to be what the world was waiting for - the invasion of Europe against the Nazi forces. Now, the feeling was unbelievable, and my prayers were for the brave men and women who were taking part in it. Our group was meant to go on D+3. However, because of channel roughness and other factors, we were held back, and our 486th Battalion and other elements of the 3rd Armored went on to Omaha Beach on June 23rd. We were moved to a marshaling area at Weymouth, England to await our departure which was to take us to Omaha Beach in France. It is my belief that elements of the 3rd Armored actually went earlier than the 23rd. Prior to our groups crossing the English Channel, we were given a farewell and good luck speech by General Montgomery of the English Army. On the 22nd of June, we boarded landing crafts (LCTs), and headed across the English Channel.

Crossing the channel was an experience that I will never forget. There was a feeling of anticipation and apprehension. My half-track was chained to the deck of the LCT to keep it from moving. There were many ships blinking code messages to each other. Barrage balloons were overhead, and as we approached the beach, there were remnants of landing crafts at the edge of the beach. We went on to and reached Omaha Beach on D+18, which had been secured thanks to the courage and valor of brave men and women of our country and our Allies - those who paid the ultimate price, those whose wounds might never heal, and those who managed to fight on, not knowing what lay ahead. We moved up that winding path you often see in the documentaries to a spot inland where we de-waterproofed our vehicles. We were now able to respond to whatever combat might break out. My radios were operable, and I was able to contact all the others in my battalion if necessary. Now, wherever we went, we were seeing the aftermath of the bloody struggle that had previously raged on the ground. In addition to discarded equipment, there were burnt vehicles, scattered corpses that had not been picked up yet, and dead cows and horses, which were mostly the casualties of German artillery. The horses were being cut up for food by civilians.

The first night after we settled into a position, a lieutenant suggested that we dig fox holes. The ground was so hard that I gave up digging. After a few minutes, there was a loud whooshing sound, one that none of us recognized. It resounded several times, and I asked the lieutenant who was nearby what were those sounds. His answer was that it was incoming mail, which meant that German artillery was coming into our field. To say the least, I was now able to dig in spite of the hard ground. However, from then on, I never dug another fox hole, as we moved so quickly, I did not want to expend the energy and then just move on without using the foxhole. I was wrong, I realize, but it worked out, as I would find a ditch, a low spot, or something in the hedge rows which would be deep enough to afford me protection. The best fox hole, which I didn't have to dig but was able to use, was the one that I came across that a German soldier had abandoned. It was substantially shored up with wood planks, dug deep, and well camouflaged.

I would like to relate a few incidents that occurred in the ensuing days in Normandy:

Once, as I stood under a tree on a very quiet sunny day when one would not even think that there was a war going on, from out of nowhere, a sniper took a shot at me. The bullet split a small branch a couple of inches from my ear, but the sniper was nowhere to be found. I had a realization that the future would probably contain many life or death incidents.

In Normandy, there was a rumor that Mongolians from Russia were fighting alongside the Germans. I understood that this was so because they were fighting with German guns at their back and thus had no choice but to face us. Some had been captured, but I had not seen them.

In one instance, German planes flew over us and dropped leaflets showing a picture of a female in a nightclub in the United States lying across a table - the caption under the picture said that she was being raped and that this might be your girlfriend or wife, and wouldn't you like to be home to protect her. Of course, this was to entice us to surrender.

Another incident in Normandy was one in which we were alerted that a gas attack was imminent. We were always supposed to be able to put our hands on a gas mask in an emergency such as we had been told was happening here. However, I could not find my gas mask at first, and by the time I did, the alert was over. Luckily for me, a little while later, it was discovered that the tremendous cloud that had appeared in the distance was not gas, but instead something that the Germans had exploded.

In Normandy, our battery commander, Captain DeFranco, pulled a man from a burning tank and saved him from death, and as a result received a silver star. Our medical team had been surrounded in the same area by Germans, and a few men from our medical team had been captured. After the war, these men were found alive in a German prison camp. I felt that they had been given special attention only because they were able to assist the Germans in their hospitals.

In addition, as a communication sergeant, I had to climb a tall tree to string a communication line and use a hand generator so that the Germans would not be able to pick up my signal. The amusing part about the whole thing was that in civilian life, I would not even climb a ladder because it would make me dizzy; however, in this situation, I had no choice.

The Falais Pocket/Gap:

In the Falais Pocket, there were thousands of Germans encircled. We and the British were involved. There were many Germans who did escape the encirclement, but also there were many captured and killed. My track was camouflaged and off to the side of a road in the pocket. I recall the sound of heavy artillery that was coming so close to our track that one did not dare to wander a few feet from it. There was much more to the story of the Falais Pocket, but I will leave that to history.

I would be remiss if I did not tell you about a newly acquired friend named Pico. Pico was a small beautiful brown and white short-haired terrier who came up to us and befriended us when my driver Greg and I were in Normandy stretched out on the ground. As I recall, Greg chose the dog's name because somehow it related to a nun in India who was called Sister Pico, and she might have actually been Greg's sister. Pico stayed with us through most of the war up to the time of the Battle of the Bulge. She was so well acclimated to the sounds of war that if the Germans were in the vicinity, I would gently hold her mouth closed so she would not bark or make a sound, which might give away our position. She would actually stay quiet until I motioned with my hand that it was alright to move and/or make a sound. That dog always stayed by my side during the entire time that she traveled with us.

Normally, Pico would relieve herself by going off somewhere, but then she would always return by the time we had to move on, whether it was for emergency move or to reposition ourselves. One day, however, when a move had to be made suddenly, Pico was nowhere nearby. Sadly, the move had to be made without her, for if we stayed behind to find her and in doing so made contact with German soldiers in the area, it could have meant the loss of lives. Going without her and leaving her behind was traumatic for us; although she was not a human, she had become a big part of our lives and brought us much comfort in difficult situations. If you are an animal lover, then you know exactly how Greg and I felt. We hoped that she was able to find some others who would love her as we did. Later on, we did acquire another dog that we named Butch. However, Butch was not with us day and night. He basically just came around to get food. The last we saw of Butch was when we were actually in the midst of a move, and he was running in back of us trying to catch up, but we could not stop for him.

St. Lo:

One of the most intense encounters I ever experienced was sitting on the edge of St. Lo while more than 2,400 bombers of all sorts were bombing St. Lo to drive out the Germans. One could hardly see the sky, as it was blocked by the enormous amount of aircraft above us. If I recall correctly, this engagement was called "Cobra" by the U.S. Army. The ground trembled as if a minor earthquake was taking place.

As I sat in my track on the perimeter of St. Lo, Captain De-Franco came up to me and asked me to "ride shotgun" in his jeep into St. Lo with him and his driver named Anctil. I sat perched in the back of the jeep with my M1 and a 30 caliber machine gun. At one point, artillery shells were coming into the city close enough to endanger us, so we had to hop out of the jeep to take shelter in the entrance way of a brick building, which reminded me of our Sheehan Center back in Bridgeport, Connecticut. While there, my mind wandered back to a time several years earlier when I sat in the Palace Theater in Bridgeport as a civilian and saw a newsreel depicting the German forces invading Poland and other countries. I just couldn't believe that I was now in the midst of that same war that I had seen on the screen.

Across the road from this building was a small house out of which came a little girl with her mother. They approached us, even though they too were in danger. In her hand, the little girl clutched a flower which she handed to me. Then she and her mother thanked us for freeing them from the Germans. Although I truly appreciated the sentiment, it was still hard for me to comprehend how they could feel thankful when all around them was destruction. I guess, though, that they had been given relief from the severe restrictions that had been imposed upon them by the Germans and hope for the future.

Within a block's range from our location, there was a jewelry shop which had its windows blown out from the bombardments. There was still jewelry such as rings and watches there for the taking. Because my dad had raised me never to take anything that did not belong to me, even though this could have been labeled the "spoils of war," I remembered my father's teaching and did not take anything. Though I was sure that someone else would come along and not be able to resist the temptation to take "the spoils of war," I felt that morally I did the right thing. Who knows, perhaps I might have taken something and then been killed five minutes later.

When Captain DeFranco relieved me of my shotgun duty, Anctil drove me back to my track, where my driver Greg and my dog Pico were waiting for me.

After the Americans had taken Paris, I recall standing in my half-track behind a 50 caliber machine gun, resentfully watching the French soldiers about a ¼ mile away going into the city. I was tired and dirty and witnessed these refreshed looking soldiers entering the city as its liberators. I understood that they were the recipients of hugs, kisses, and wine and were allowed to go into the city first so that General DeGaulle would receive the credit for freeing Paris.

The Evening Before Heading for the Roer River:

The day before we were to head for the Roer River, I had consumed some whiskey given to a few of us by one of the lieutenants. As a communication sergeant, it was my responsibility to make sure that all the radios in my Battery C were working properly in case of emergencies arising with our other tracks. Somewhere in the late afternoon, my radio technician, Harold Barlow, told me that one radio was not operating properly, and it would not be able to be fixed in time for the drive. Hearing of this, I notified Captain DeFranco, and he immediately summoned me to his makeshift command post. Before I went, a lieutenant gave me another shot of whiskey to give me strength upon facing the captain, and I was feeling pretty good. Greg, my track driver, got a jeep, and off we went on a rickety drive to see Captain DeFranco to explain to him what was going on. Upon arrival, I entered the makeshift command post, approached the captain unsteadily, and saluted him. In as steady a voice as I could muster, I explained how Barlow was not able to fix the radio now, but that he would be able to do so given a little more time. I assume, because of my condition, Captain

DeFranco's response was "Sergeant, I trust you, and that is why you are in charge. We'll just make sure that another track is close so that messages can be relayed." With that said, he told me to relax, and then he offered me a drink. It was a half a glass of scotch, and he poured himself one also. Now, you must know that an order is an order, and so I complied. As the old saying goes, "I needed that like I needed a hole in the head."

Now that my mission was accomplished, I stood up, saluted the captain, and unsteadily walked out of the makeshift CP. Greg was waiting for me, I flopped into the jeep, and back we went to our track which was sitting alongside an empty flower hot house which had a small office attached to it. The floor of the office was concrete, and there I found a young man sitting on his duffel bag with other gear alongside of him. I had not met him before, and he explained that he was a replacement for one of the men we had lost. He said that his last name was Michaud and his home was in the state of Maine. He told me that he had not experienced any combat, and as we sat there, he explained how he had been in the Navy and was involved in the fire at the Coconut Grove Night Club in Boston a few years earlier. He said he had pulled several people to safety. He went on to say that after his term ended in the Navy, he decided to remain in the military by joining the Army.

As we were speaking, we could hear the sounds of artillery and guns going off in the distance. Michaud was obviously very nervous, as this was his first night in combat, and I calmed him down with explanations of all the sounds. He then pulled out his wallet and showed me a picture of his wife and children. Greg, Michaud, and I tried to get some sleep on the concrete floor before dawn, which was not far off.

With the dawn came sounds of planes and artillery. We awakened and had to await a march order which came a short while later on the heels of a driving rain storm. I stood up in the front of my track wearing a radio headset and manned the 50 caliber machine gun at the front of the track while the driving rain pelted me in the face. To this day, when I am driving on a major highway and there is a heavy rainstorm, as the rain hits the windshield, I always have a flashback of the drive to the Roer River.

Braisne and Soissons:

My track, 3-Baker, was second in a column headed by an M15 commanded by Hollis Butler and his crew. As it was going down a slight hill into a small town called Braisne, a German troop train was pulling into the center of town. To the right of our column, there was a tall steeple from which we were receiving sniper fire. Butler's M15 firing power was a 37 millimeter cannon and two 50 caliber machine guns. He turned his 37 millimeter cannon toward the steeple and shot and silenced the snipers. Then he directed his 50 caliber machine guns at the train, killing many German soldiers who were firing weapons from the train windows. Next, turning his machine guns and his 37 millimeter cannon toward the train's engine, he blew it up. There were two tiger tanks on flatbeds behind the engine, and German soldiers, firing weapons at us as they left the train, were trying to get to the tanks which were operable. They did not get to their destinations, as they were raked with machine gun fire. While all this was taking place, there were many civilians in the streets milling around, ignoring the fact that there was gunfire going on and that they were subject to being hit. Miraculously, I saw only one civilian casualty, a civilian sitting on the ground with his back against a tree, holding one of his arms which was bleeding. There were many Germans killed in the heavy gunfire that had been directed at the train, and many were taken prisoners.

Me, after a 10 mile run, and Hamilton McQueen about to go on guard

Me and another soldier coming down a rope ladder in basic training

Corporal Milton Cohen giving instructions to a group on self defense (I am first on left)

Me and some of my army buddies on a Sunday morning at Camp Davis
(l to r: Weir, me, Gagnon, and McQueen)

Four Bridgeport buddies in a bomb crater in
Normandy (Top Row, l to r: Ron Condon,
Cono DeSarli; Bottom Row,
l to r: Me, Bruno DiNapoli)

Me, relaxing with a cigarette in hand
in Normandy

Me, in Normandy, in a well dug evacuated German foxhole

Harold Barlow from Indiana, who was vital in keeping my radios running

Belgian free underground fighters

Pico, my faithful companion, perching on my shoulders and chest, who was with me from Normandy up to the Battle of the Bulge, where I lost him due to sudden troop movement

Me, posing with my crew on 3-Baker
(l to r: Moffitt, Barlow, me, and Gregoire; in back, Urbanski)

Kornelimunster - l to r: Lucia, Bouchard, Logue (who was killed by a loose bomb falling from a plane a short while after the picture was taken), Little, Brigante, and me

Remains of human bodies at Nordhausen Concentration Camp in Germany

Troop Review after war

COL DUNNINGTON
PRES. TRUMAN GENERAL HICKEY 486ᵗʰ TROOPS

The 486th Bn. Troops about to be reviewed by President Truman (photo depicts President Truman on left, General Hickey in center, and our Battalion Commander, Colonel Dunnington on right)

Celebrity Ingrid Bergman
visiting 3rd Armored Division
in Darmstadt, Germany and
signing autographs

Ed Cohen and I go to Heidelberg, Germany
on a weekend pass

Celebrity Bob Hope and professional fighter Billy Conn (who had fought Joe Louis) visit
troops in Darmstadt, Germany

486th Battalion M16s, on the road to Darmstadt, lined up, waiting for review by President Truman

Colonel Dunnington shakes hands with President Truman

Major General Maurice Rose -
3rd Armored Division commander

Captain DeFranco, Battery C
commander, with his driver Anctil.

Colonel Dunnington with General Omar Bradley

Me, operating my radios in my track

Me, holding a stray dog in Wixhausen

The Siegfried Line - a German defense system, almost 400 miles long, with bunkers, tunnels, and tank traps, built to repel the entry of enemy tanks into German territory

Me and Cono DeSarli, the 3rd Armored Division Middleweight Champion, about 20 years after the end of the war

My wife Molly Levine Swirsky and me on our wedding day, November 24, 1945

Me and my wife Molly at an army reunion in Enfield, Connecticut

Return visit to Europe in 1994 (l to r: Me, St. Amour, Eicke, Simon, O'Brien, Goodie, Eckman, unknown person; background on left: Sullivan)

Three army couples get together in Mystic, Connecticut
(the Pomerleau, Swirskys, and St. Amours)

MÉDAILLE DU JUBILÉ

René GARREC, Président du Conseil Régional de Basse-Normandie

décerne à **Robert SWIRSKY**

La Médaille Commémorative du Cinquantième Anniversaire du débarquement et de la bataille
de Normandie, en reconnaissance de la part qu'il a prise à la libération de la Région, de la France et de l'Europe.

Le Président du Conseil Régional

Abbaye aux Dames, ce Lundi 5 Septembre 1994

René GARREC

In the 1990s, army buddy Jim Cavanaugh and his wife Elaine return
to the grounds of Hays House in England

Only this text in English is authoritative

ACT OF MILITARY SURRENDER

1. We the undersigned, acting by authority of the German High Command, hereby surrender unconditionally to the Supreme Commander, Allied Expeditionary Force and simultaneously to the Soviet High Command all forces on land, sea, and in the air who are at this date under German control.

2. The German High Command will at once issue orders to all German military, naval and air authorities and to all forces under German control to cease active operations at 2301 hours Central European time on 8 May and to remain in the positions occupied at that time. No ship, vessel, or aircraft is to be scuttled, or any damage done to their hull, machinery or equipment.

3. The German High Command will at once issue to the appropriate commanders, and ensure the carrying out of any further orders issued by the Supreme Commander, Allied Expeditionary Force and by the Soviet High Command.

4. This act of military surrender is without prejudice to, and will be superseded by any general instrument of surrender imposed by, or on behalf of the United Nations and applicable to GERMANY and the German armed forces as a whole.

5. In the event of the German High Command or any of the forces under their control failing to act in accordance with this Act of Surrender, the Supreme Commander, Allied Expeditionary Force and the Soviet High Command will take such punitive or other action as they deem appropriate.

Signed at *Rheims* at *0241* on the 7<u>th</u> day of May, 1945.
France

On behalf of the German High Command.

[signature: Jodl]

IN THE PRESENCE OF

On behalf of the Supreme Commander,
Allied Expeditionary Force.

[signature: W. B. Smith]

On behalf of the Soviet
High Command.

[signature]

[signature] -2-

Major General, French Army
(Witness)

[signature]

SUPREME HEADQUARTERS
ALLIED EXPEDITIONARY FORCE

TO ALL MEMBERS OF THE ALLIED EXPEDITIONARY FORCE:

The task which we set ourselves is finished, and the time has come for me to relinquish Combined Command.

In the name of the United States and the British Commonwealth, from whom my authority is derived, I should like to convey to you the gratitude and admiration of our two nations for the manner in which you have responded to every demand that has been made upon you. At times, conditions have been hard and the tasks to be performed arduous. No praise is too high for the manner in which you have surmounted every obstacle.

I should like, also, to add my own personal word of thanks to each one of you for the part you have played, and the contribution you have made to our joint victory.

Now that you are about to pass to other spheres of activity, I say Good-bye to you and wish you Good Luck and God-Speed.

Dwight D Eisenhower

To you who answered the call of your country and served in its Armed Forces to bring about the total defeat of the enemy, I extend the heartfelt thanks of a grateful Nation. As one of the Nation's finest, you undertook the most severe task one can be called upon to perform. Because you demonstrated the fortitude, resourcefulness and calm judgment necessary to carry out that task, we now look to you for leadership and example in further exalting our country in peace.

Harry Truman

THE WHITE HOUSE

The humorous part of this incident, if one can imagine that there might be such a thing in this serious situation, was that a woman was running around handing tomatoes to a few of us amidst the chaos. I guess this was her way of thanking us for fighting the enemy.

As this sudden and unexpected incident came to an end, we pulled out and left members of our division to mop up. Departing via the dirt road which led out of town, German aircraft appeared and hovered over us. However, before they could do us any harm, our M15s and M16s drove them off. We continued toward our destination for several hours, and close to midnight, we pulled into a wooded area for the night. There was no moon, and the night was pitch black. As I had to observe radio silence after 11 p.m. and only use the radios in a dire emergency, I told my driver Greg to get some sleep and that I would stand guard. While I walked around the track several times, there was a burst of machine gun fire from the opposite side of the dirt road which just cleared the top of my head. We had apparently moved into an area where Germans were located a short distance away and across the road. Since they heard our movement into the woods, they were apparently firing at random, hoping to hit somebody. Even though we had an M16 near us, we did not return fire, so as not to give away our position.

As daylight approached, division armored infantry took care of the situation and cleaned out the Germans.

My Parents Learn of my Whereabouts:

Whenever I sent a letter home, I always made sure I wrote in a way that would give my parents the impression that I was not in any real danger, as I did not want to worry them. However, eventually they were to discover that my letters did not tell the whole truth. I will explain how that happened.

When the Jewish "High Holidays" came in September of 1944, myself and two other Jewish boys of the 486th Battalion were notified that a holiday service would be held in a field not too far away. If we wished to attend the service, we would be picked up by a truck and taken to it. We chose to attend, and found that there were other soldiers at the service who I assume were also from the 3rd Armored Division. We were given prayer books, and a clergyman of our faith led us through the service. Nearby, watching the proceedings, was a news reporter from a Chicago news syndicate. He approached us (Bob Swirsky, Nate Laden, and Edward Cohen) and told us that he was there for the primary purpose of getting interviews from Jewish soldiers attending their holiday services. The interviews were published in the Chicago newspapers and also sent to the New York Jewish Forward where they were published within a week from the time of the interviews. The day the articles appeared in the New York newspaper, my father was taking his daily walk down Madison Avenue in Bridgeport. There was a little candy store whose owner, Mrs. Berkowitz, was sitting in front of the store. My father knew her well, as we had been neighbors years before. As a matter of fact, she had known me since I was born. She called my father over to her as he passed by and asked whether he had seen the Forward that day. When he responded that he had not seen it, she pointed out the article that said that three tankers (Bob Swirsky, Nate Laden, and Edward Cohen) from Bridgeport, Connecticut were attending services in a field underneath trees while the war was taking place with wounded soldiers being carried away on stretchers, heavy artillery sounds, etc. In other words, the report described a scene so horrific that my father had tears rolling down his cheeks when he read the article. (I learned this when I came home from the war and spoke with Mrs. Berkowitz, and she told me all the details about my dad reading the article and his reaction to it.) Now he knew that I was not out of danger but instead was in combat zones and subject to harm.

I did not mind the fact that the reporter wrote this column. However, I felt that there was no need to put the blood and guts details in it, as there was none of that at the high holiday service. I guess, though, that it made for good reading, and after all, that type of reporting does sell newspapers.

23 Engineers Turn into 28 Potential Combatants:

One very dark night, when my track stopped for the night, we found ourselves in a farm yard in France. Around us were a few cows, which made it very treacherous to lie down and stretch our limbs on the ground because there might have been cow pads. (There had been instances during the war, especially in Normandy, where a soldier would lie down on the ground and find that his head was not on a pillow, but instead on a cow pad - ugh!) We were alerted by some GIs, who had spotted us as they passed by so closely that they couldn't help but see us, that there were Germans coming our way. The GIs could not tell us how many there were, but the way they spoke, it sounded like we would have a battle on our hands if spotted. Apparently, the GIs did not want to get involved and went on their way. Now, the five of us had to figure out what we would do if we were confronted by the Germans. Out of the five of us, four wished to give up. Not that I was so much braver than them, but I took the stand that we should fight it out, as I felt that if we were taken prisoners, we would be killed anyway. I believed that with 30 caliber and 50 caliber machine guns and our own individual guns, we could put up one "helluva" battle. However, I could not convince the others to change their minds. Incidentally, one of the four others was a lieutenant, who I would never have imagined would want to surrender.

A short while later, a tremendous army vehicle pulled up near us on the side of the road. It was a group of engineers who might have been going somewhere to put up a bridge or something of that nature. They told us that there were 23 of them. After we related to them what might happen in the ensuing hours, they said that if it should occur, they would join us in the battle. Now, seeing that there were 28 of us, the other four men agreed to concede to my wishes and not surrender.

As it turned out, I was grateful that the Germans who were approaching us went around us quite a distance away, not realizing that we were in a nearby field.

A small anecdote regarding my feelings about engagement with the Germans on this particular occasion or any others during the course of the war:

I vowed that I would never surrender if it came down to the wire. I always carried an extra bullet in my cartridge belt so I, not the enemy, could be in charge of my own demise. Thank goodness, I never was confronted with that decision.

Mons, Belgium:

In the area of Mons, there was extremely heavy fighting going on. My track was situated on the outskirts of the city, and I was kept very busy with transmissions on my radio. The result of the fighting in Mons was that thousands of Germans were killed and thousands were taken prisoners. It was a battle regarded as one which would certainly affect the outcome of the war.

Kornelimunster:

Somewhere around 10:45 at night in the town of Kornelimunster, I was sitting in my track and felt a heavy thud which lifted my dog Pico and me slightly up off our seats. I looked out from under the canvas which always covered me when I operated my radios. The sight I beheld was flares coming down from the sky and lighting up the area as bright as if it were a night baseball game at Yankee Stadium. German planes were swooping in and out and dropping bombs. I had not yet observed my radio silence which would come only 15 minutes later at 11 p.m. I had to make a decision whether or not to get on my radio, make contact with an M16 close by, and tell them to open fire. Before I could decide, the corporal in charge of the M16 contacted me and asked me whether he could retaliate. Given that we were entirely visible to the planes that were dropping the bombs, I felt that we should return fire. My response to the corporal was "Let them have it!" even though we were not to fire after dark, as we would give away our position.

The whole situation was hectic. Greg and I got out of our track and watched what was going on, despite the fact that our lives were being jeopardized. As we stood there, Captain DeFranco came racing up to us, threw his helmet on the ground, and shouted "Who the heck gave orders to fire?" I responded "I did, sir." He then asked me why. I said simply, "The area was lit up as if it were daylight, so I felt that we had the right to respond." As we and other 486th anti-aircraft guns opened fire in the area, so did other anti-aircraft guns in the VII Corps. It was disclosed the next day that several planes were brought down.

The next morning when things had quieted down, I was called before Major Walker, and he asked me what had happened. I repeated the whole incident, and he told me that he was not going to pass judgment on my decision. However, he said that because the occurrence took place after dark, he could not make the final decision as to what the consequences would be, as technically I had gone against procedures. The next person to pass judgment was a general who had been told about the battle. He said that I had done the right thing, as we were completely visible, and that if the same type of thing were to happen again, I would be correct in opening fire.

The next evening was damp and cold, and I was freezing. Jim Robinson, one of our medics, said "I have just the solution, Bob." He gave me a drink which warmed me up and made my hair stand up and my toes curl. I asked, "Jim, what did you give me?" He answered that it was medic's alcohol spiked with pineapple juice. Shortly after, I was offered a three day pass which would enable me to go to Verviers, Belgium. This would be the only time I would get away from a combat zone during my 323 days of fighting in the division. As another soldier by the name of Roberge was also given a pass, we stayed together in Verviers. One evening, we went to an underground restaurant where food and drinks were served. Sitting at the tables were many GIs accompanied by females. In one of the corners, I recognized a friend from the States sitting with an attractive young lady. Knowing that he had a wife back home with whom I had attended and graduated high school, I wondered whether he was having an affair. So as not to embarrass him, I did not approach him. I just walked by his table and winked, and no words were spoken between us. After the war was over and I was back in the States, I had the opportunity to talk to my friend's brother. His brother told me that he had been in charge of a USO group which entertained the soldiers, so evidently, the female accompanying him was part of the group.

On those nights we spent in Verviers, Roberge and I stayed in a Red Cross building and actually got the opportunity to sleep in beds with sheets and blankets, a comfort we had not experienced in a very long time. We also were able to spend some time in reputable bars and enjoy drinking some good ale. As nice as our time was in Verviers, when we returned to our battery, it seemed like we had never left.

In the area of Kornelimunster, we lost three men - Logue, Pellici, and Nowicki. Nowicki had been a replacement from Brooklyn and had just joined us a short while before. It was most unfortunate because I believe it was a "friendly" bomb that took their lives. One of our planes that was carrying two 500 lb. bombs was flying overhead when one of the bombs became loose and came down in our area. One moment I was talking to Logue, and two minutes later, he was dead. The fragments also killed Pellici and Nowicki. Another soldier killed was a 67th Field Artillery man who was quite a distance from the incident. It was amazing that the fragment that killed him traveled so far.

Two relatively minor casualties involved Briganti (whose home was in Norwalk, Connecticut) and Palazzo (who came from Massachusetts). They were standing nearby and were knocked to the ground by the tremor, shook up, and dazed. I was fortunate to not have been affected by the event. What made the experience especially sad was that Logue was not wearing a helmet; if he had been, he might have lived, as his death was the result of being hit on the top of the head by the fragments.

Ardennes - The Battle of the Bulge:

It was late evening when I received a message that I was to put a grenade launcher on my M1 and my crew and I were to dig a ditch alongside of our tracks. I did not get to do either, however, as right after this request was made, sometime around 2 a.m. in the morning, a march order was given and there was not time to carry it out. Soon the tanks near us started their engines and began moving out. Our track and others in our group followed. The sound of the revving engines and the movement of the tanks gave me an awesome feeling.

Toward morning, we ended our drive in the vicinity of St. Vith and Houfalaize. We pulled into a position next to a field where a lieutenant had set up a small CP (command post). I asked the lieutenant what was going on, and he told me that the Germans were attempting a break-through in great numbers. I asked him where they were at that moment, and he answered that they were about two miles up the road. I, in turn, asked what our chances were of holding them. He reassured me that we had so much armor to confront them that we should be able to hold. Rumor had it that when dawn broke, a tree that I had walked under when I went to report to the lieutenant had harbored snipers in it. Although I had escaped being hit by them because the snipers did not see me, a couple of other GIs were not so lucky.

Greg and I brought our track into a little town called Juzaine. It was situated not too far from Bastogne. There was a small hotel there, and the owners allowed us to set up part of our radio equipment in the hotel lobby. Opposite the hotel was a farmhouse where a young lady named Annette and her parents lived. They befriended us for the short time that we were there and suggested that we could rest in a loft in their barn, but we did not accept their offer, as the situation in the area was critical.

During the Battle of the Bulge, the weather was so bitterly cold that if I was holding my mess kit without wearing gloves, it would actually pull off skin from my fingers. Speaking of the difficult weather conditions brings to mind the brave men and women, the other armored units, medics, and especially the infantry, and all others who found the strength to stave off the enemy under the immeasurable odds of freezing cold and snowy conditions. They fought so gallantly with tremendous numbers of them being wounded and losing their lives.

On Christmas Day, the sky began to clear, which enabled our bombers to fly again. I watched as several went over my head with our fighter planes flying beneath them as protective cover. All of a sudden, from out of the sky above the bombers, German planes swooped down. Apparently, these planes were not detected, as they came out of the bright sunlight. As I remember, a few of the bombers (I believe that they were B17s) were hit, though I do not know what happened to the crews, as they came down a distance away. Over time, my memory of this incident faded, but my mind became clear about it once again when years later, I read an article about another soldier, who, during an interview, talked about having the same experience as I did.

Nordhausen:

As my track came into Nordhausen, I pulled up alongside what appeared to be a page fence. On the other side of the fence, I observed a stack of bodies piled on top of each other like cord wood. The compound, which proved to be a concentration camp, had already been entered by other 3rd Armored soldiers who had put a stop to the atrocities which had been taking place there. I left my track to go into the compound and entered an area which contained dead bodies of men, women, and children lying all over the place. The space had a roof over it, probably about 10 feet high. After many years, I thought that shack-like area was something about which I had dreamed. However, in going through a 3rd Armored Division book, there was an actual picture of this same place, so I knew that it was real.

There was a little girl's body in the shack amongst the other bodies which was emaciated, and the image of her has not left my mind after all these years. Another image that has never left me is of an old man leaning back against a tree wearing a heavy army-type hat and coat. I tried to give him something to eat, but he couldn't open his mouth, and when I talked to him, he could only respond by blinking his eyes. Not knowing at this point that this place was a concentration camp, I just couldn't fathom that man could be so inhumane. All that I could think of was that this place was the property of a mortician who never interred his bodies, but instead just threw them into the area and left them there. Also, around the camp, there were others wandering about in a dazed state of mind.

A short distance from the actual concentration camp was a tunnel which led to a very deep underground factory called Camp Dora. The slave laborers of the camp were making V-bombs under close supervision by the Germans. If they came up from the tunnel after a night's work so exhausted that they were no longer considered of any use, it would become their death warrant. This information was given to me when I returned to Nordhausen in 1994 with members of the 3rd Armored Division. The Germans who were in charge of the camp, which was now, of course, a most solemn place where one could hear a pin drop, told us that about 32 people were hanged daily because they could not perform anymore.

We did not stay long at the camp after it was liberated, however a quorum of soldiers was left behind to take charge and to make sure that the Germans would be made to bury the bodies.

Dessau:

While heavy fighting was going on in the city of Dessau, my track and a couple of M16s were in a field a few miles away.

You would hardly know the war was going on nearby, as our area was so quiet. In the middle of our field was a tank which needed repairs.

Throughout the war, I never got any real sleep because I had to sleep with one eye open and my ears attuned to the radio. It was so quiet in this field, however, that I decided perhaps I could catch a nap. I took out a sleeping bag that was packed away in my track (which, incidentally, I had not used since bivouacs in the States). As I never took off my clothes to sleep through the entire war, I climbed into the bag fully dressed. I put my M1, eyeglasses, and helmet on the ground within reach and zipped the bag closed. As fate would have it, I would not get any sleep because before I could settle in, I heard noises that sounded like rifle fire. I tried to open the sleeping bag to detect what was going on; however, the zipper would not open. Probably, a thread was caught in it. Out of sheer desperation, I ripped open the bag, and as I lay on the ground, I stuck out my head without lifting it up, as rifle fire was coming in my direction. What I saw in the distance were German soldiers dismounting from bicycles and running toward us, firing at us at the same time. I managed to transmit our predicament to our battery commander, who offered to have artillery turned around toward the oncoming Germans. I told him that would mean that we would also be hit and that it was not feasible, as we had the situation under control because of our fire power. All this seemed to be happening in a split second.

There were only 48 of us in this field, and we later found out that there was almost a full company of German soldiers who had attacked us. Even though we were greatly outnumbered, we had our M16s with 50 caliber machine guns and one mess truck in the center of the field also with a 50 caliber machine gun, while the Germans had only rifles and bazookas. So although they had the numbers, we had the fire power of 50 calibers throwing out over 600 rounds a minute; therefore, it was no contest.

Eventually, it was determined that we had destroyed a company of Germans who had broken away from their units and were trying to get back to their lines. Among those captured were young Hitler youths who appeared to be 15 and 16 year old boys. Most of them had been wounded and were bleeding and crying. They were herded onto trucks and taken away.

This entire incident might never have occurred if it hadn't been for a lieutenant and his driver who had decided to reconnoiter the area and consequently had been spotted by German soldiers who were cutting across the farthest part of the field, at least 300 feet away. The German soldiers directed fire at the lieutenant's jeep. The driver was killed, but the lieutenant escaped. Then the German soldiers spotted us and attacked.

Furlough After Dessau Attack:

After the unexpected confrontation with the company of German infantry at Dessau, Captain DeFranco offered me a furlough. I had not been granted one back in the States as many others had after Louisiana Maneuvers. After coming as close to my maker as I just had at any other time during the war, I decided to take it. I could have gone to any of the places which were now occupied by the Allied forces. I considered France, Belgium, Italy, and Switzerland, but I decided that it would be nice to go back to England to see all the friends I had made while training there prior to "D Day," and to let them know that I had made it through the war thus far. When I made this decision, I did not know that the war would end four days later. I gathered my things together, and before I knew it, I was on my way to Paris, Le Havre, and across the Channel to England.

The war ended while I was on the Channel. I would have loved to have been in Paris when the war ended and the news was announced; however, when I wound up in London, I was warmly greeted by the English public. Prior to my leaving on the furlough, Lou Ferrigno, the barber who had given us the GI haircuts in basic training, took me aside and gave me the address of his cousins who lived in London. He said he would appreciate it if I would contact them and told me that I would not regret it.

The first night in London, feeling very lonely, I headed for Ferrigno's cousin's address. Arriving there shortly after midnight, I found myself facing a restaurant. I rang a resounding doorbell to announce myself to the owners of the glass front establishment. A woman peered through the curtain on the door, and seeing a soldier, she was apparently not afraid to let me enter. Immediately upon introducing myself and mentioning her cousin's name, she invited me to come in and asked whether or not I had eaten that evening. As I had not eaten, she sat me down and insisted upon preparing a meal, even at that late hour, which consisted of steak and potatoes. What a treat that was for me after not having eaten a steak since I had left the States!

While I was eating, her husband entered the room, and both of them, after hearing some of my story of my participation in the war, asked how their cousin Lou was doing. They then asked me whether I had a place to sleep that night. Their home was above the restaurant. When I answered in the negative, they insisted that I stay with them for the night, and longer if I wished. I told them that I would appreciate it for that evening but that I had much to do with only ten days to see all my friends at the various places where I had trained in England.

I did not know that they had a teenage daughter and that I would be sleeping in her room, which would mean that she would have to sleep elsewhere. I did not want to take their daughter's room; however, they insisted, and I wound up in a large, plush bed fit for a king! Morning came, and I was treated to a bacon and eggs breakfast, and after a few hugs and my thanks, I departed. The couple directed me to a train station, where I boarded a train to Wiltshire, which was where we had been billeted in the Quonset huts in Hays House before the invasion.

I immediately headed for East Noyle, where the girls who lived in the Bothy House had treated us so kindly in our training days. The only one missing amongst the 11 girls was Goldina, the girl with whom I had established a great friendship and who had been writing to me during the war. The girls at the Bothy House told me that she had gone back to her home in London, and at that moment, I looked forward to seeing her in London, as I would be returning there. The girls put me up for the night in the hallway on a cot, although it was against the house rules. They had to be careful because as I have earlier stated, there was a mistress who supervised the girls and enforced the rules.

In the early morning, I headed for the pub where I had made friends with the pub owner and his wife prior to our departure from Hays House. They were very happy to see that I had survived the war and made me a hot breakfast and asked me many questions about the others in my outfit who also had become their friends.

From the pub, I went back to London. I rode on a two-decker bus and sat next to a gentleman who spoke Cockney English. As he talked to me, I could not understand one word that he was saying. For all I knew, he could have been saying negative things about me, but I nodded my head in agreement to everything he said. When I arrived at Goldina's home, which was in an apartment house complex, her sister Rose greeted me at the door and told me that Goldina was not there. (Years later, I found out that Goldina had gone to live with her brother in Brazil.) However, since I was already there, I invited Rose to spend the afternoon with me, and we went to a movie, which I believe was "The Postman Rings Twice" with Lana Turner.

The next afternoon, while walking in the area of 10 Downing Street, I met a young school teacher, and we spent a few hours together. There was a crowd gathering, and the young lady told me that it was probably due to somebody of importance who was about to appear on the balcony of 10 Downing Street. Sure enough, out came Winston Churchill who addressed the crowd. He praised the British soldiers for their accomplishments in the war, but in my estimation, did not give any real praise to the Americans and other Allies. I complained to my friend, and she responded "Don't feel bad. You have to realize that he is speaking to a British audience."

With my furlough coming to an end, I had to get back to a U.S. information headquarters in Paris, and they would tell me approximately where my battalion was now stationed in Germany. As the war was over, the 486th Battalion of the 3rd Armored Division was now an occupation force. I was put on a 2 ½ ton truck with other soldiers, and we headed toward Germany. After a long ride, we reached the vicinity of Darmstadt, Germany, where I was dropped off at a street corner and told that according to their map, I would find the 486th Battalion in that area. There I was, standing on a street corner on the main road to Darmstadt and looking down a side street. As it seemed that the only way to go was down that street, that is where I went. Walking along with my barracks bag slung over my shoulder, I never felt lonelier in my entire life. I trudged along past many houses while people sitting on the porches stared at me. Trying to read their minds, I felt very uncomfortable because after all, even though the war was over, I had been the enemy.

Soon I spotted a soldier with his rifle on his shoulder pacing back and forth on a corner which I was approaching. If I remember correctly, the soldier was Roland St. Amour from my battery. I felt relieved just to see a familiar face. He told me that our battalion was stationed nearby, and I found out from Battery C Headquarters that I would be sleeping in the very first house on the block occupied by my driver Greg. The name of the town that we were occupying was Wixhausen, and Batterys A, B, and D, and Battalion Headquarters were not far away.

One morning, an order was issued that all vehicles were to be spotlessly cleaned because we were going to be reviewed by President Truman and other high ranking Army officers. The entire battalion was to stand in review in full dress uniform in front of our individual vehicles on the road leading to Darmstadt. On the day of review, as we stood in formation with our officers standing in front of the battalion, a couple of vehicles pulled up. Out stepped President Truman, General Hickey, and their aides. (Although I did not see him, I was told that General Eisenhower was also in the area.) Our battalion commander, Colonel Dunnington, greeted them, and they, in turn, acknowledged our battalion officers. As I stood there, I thought to myself what a tremendous honor it was to see these persons who had played such a great role in the victory over Germany.

An Unexpected Visitor:

It was a pleasant Saturday afternoon in Wixhausen when Battery C received an unexpected visitor. Wixhausen apparently had once been a train station stop. The building which was now being used as a mess hall was previously the place where people bought their tickets and waited for their trains. During our occupation of Wixhausen, passenger trains did not stop there;

it seemed that just box cars carrying freight would come through. One Saturday afternoon, though, the train stopped and a young lady got off the train. I presume the engineer was aware that she was on the train and stopped to leave her off. She approached a guard of ours who was on the corner and told him that she was very hungry. She asked whether we could give her some food and some lodging for the night, and we told her that we could, although we did not ask any officers for permission. As news traveled fast among the men, they were very anxious to see her. She was given a bed on the first floor of a house on the corner of the block. Sunday morning came, and there was a service being held at the small town's community center a short distance away. The Lutheran minister in charge of the service did not have many people in attendance. Therefore, before he started the service, he came to Battery C's area, and beginning at the other end of the block from where the girl was staying, he went to each house, hoping to recruit an audience for his Sunday service. The last house he came upon was the one where the girl was sleeping. He was intercepted by a guard standing in front of the entrance in case an officer showed up so that he could signal those inside. The guard told the minister that there was no one in the house. The soldier gave a sigh of relief as the minister accepted what he said and left. The kitchen in the house had several men sitting around, wanting to see the girl. It looked like a waiting room in a doctor's office. Once the minister was out of sight, the kitchen emptied out in a hurry. The girl woke up and was given breakfast. Though she didn't speak English, we communicated with her as best we could and learned that she had been a member of the Nazi party. Since the Nazis had lost the war, she was homeless and had nowhere to go. Immediately after she ate, she left, not to be seen again.

Christine:

Christine (I don't know why we called her Christine, as her real name was Matilda) lived in a small house next door to Greg and me. Though the war was formally over, fraternization with German frauleins was still not allowed. However, as our yards were back to back, Christine and I would often talk to each other over the fence. I spoke enough broken German to communicate with her. Our friendship grew, and eventually she invited me into her small, modest flat on the second floor of the house in which she lived. We would eat together occasionally, and she loved to make me kartofel (potato) soup. As she worked during the day in the fields where one of the things grown was sweet corn, she would bring home the largest corn that I had ever seen. She told me that the German people did not eat corn, but fed it to their farm animals. For the record, our friendship was always purely platonic. It seemed that Christine was married and that her husband had been a German fighter pilot who had reportedly been shot down in White Russia. On the mantel place in her dining room were letters, all marked MIA (missing in action). I am proud to say that because of our platonic friendship, should her husband ever have come home unexpectedly, Christine could say that she had done nothing but talked with American soldiers and that she had remained faithful to him.

In Wixhausen, there was a meeting hall that people used for functions such as dances, movies, and various town meetings. We GIs were allowed to attend the functions, as the fraternization rules were not being enforced and seemed to be dissolving. At a dance, I would socialize with Christine, but because fraternization rules were still technically in effect, I would not walk her home. Instead, we would agree to meet at her home after the dance was over. Christine's teenage brother would also attend these events. When it came time to leave the hall, whether it was because I danced with his sister, or possibly because he was proud that he had made a friend of me, an American soldier, he would leave the dance by my side. To get rid of him so that he would not know where I was going, I had to walk around the block and pretend to go into the house that Greg and I occupied. Then I would have to go over the fence to see Christine.

One evening, as we had just finished eating and were chatting, Christine asked me whether or not it was true that concentration camps existed. During the early part of the war, Christine worked in a factory with a Jewish girl whom she hid in her cellar. The girl had made Christine aware of how the Jews were being persecuted. At one point, the girl told Christine how things were getting worse for the Jewish people and that if the Germans searched houses and found her hidden in the cellar, Christine would suffer the same fate that would befall her. Consequently, the girl insisted that she leave the home to protect Christine.

I asked Christine how she could not have known about the concentration camps. She showed me her radio, which was similar to the old style Philcos that we had in the States, and told me how no matter where she turned the dial, she received only one station. That station broadcasted only Hitler's propaganda. Throughout the conversation, Christine cried as she learned the whole story of Nazi persecution of Jewish men, women, and children.

Now I would like to tell you about an embarrassing situation. Because a soldier had been castrated in a German village, we were instructed never to go out unless we went in pairs. In Wixhausen, and I am sure in all the occupied zones as well, there was to be a tight secret search in most of the territories. The search was for knives and weapons of all sorts which could do harm to the soldiers. Due to the level of secrecy, those who were to be involved were not told about it until the last possible moment. As a matter of fact, just hours before the search, I, being a sergeant, and other non coms in our battalion, were given crews of five men. At precisely 5 a.m., each crew was to go house to house in their designated area, knock on the doors, wake the people, enter their homes even if they had to do so forcibly, and search the houses thoroughly, including and especially the bureau drawers. It was just my luck that the first house I had to enter was Christine's. It meant I would have to empty the drawers that contained her underclothes. She looked at me as if to say "Robert, you know that I would not be hiding anything," but said it with an understanding smile. There were times when Christine would show her loyalty to me by her actions. In the middle of the night, I might be called to go out with Greg to investigate a robbery or a rape. I was called primarily because I spoke some German (in fact, I was called the "Burgemeister" in the village) and also because we were the occupiers and we had jurisdiction over certain events, criminal or otherwise. Christine would hear Greg pull up the jeep alongside of our house and would surmise that I was going out on an important and possibly dangerous call. She would not go to sleep until I got back, and when I did return, she would be in the window and would ask me whether I would like some tea, even though it was well after midnight. Incidentally, Christine had a sister who always referred to me as the "Shvartze Ziguener" (which meant black gypsy) because of my black hair.

Stuttgart Prison:

After serving our occupation term in Wixhausen, we were given another assignment and transferred to Stuttgart, Germany to take charge of a prison camp which held approximately 200 women. These prisoners had been active in the Nazi party under Hitler. They were confined to long barracks. There were nuns at the prison to supervise the women and to make sure that there was no interaction with the soldiers. The women were not allowed to have curtains on their windows so that they were always visible, as prisoners always had to be watched in regard to their activities. During the day, the women were allowed to go outside to exercise or get some fresh air for a few hours. Because some of the women would sunbathe topless and/or flirt with the soldiers as they stood guard in the barracks, the nuns would take away many of their privileges.

Halle Prison:

Soon after this tour of duty ended, I was sent along with four others to the town of Halle to take charge of a different prison camp. This camp did not have as many prisoners as there were at Stuttgart, but it housed both women and men. As a sergeant, I was the highest ranking person in charge of my group. There were also nuns who were brought in every time a new group of detainees arrived so that when the women prisoners went through the necessary physicals, the nuns could make sure that nothing unethical occurred.

The Halle prisoners were fed their meals through slots in their doors whereby a tray of food was pushed through the openings. They apparently were more dangerous than the prisoners that we previously had charge of in Stuttgart. They were guarded very closely and were allowed only a very short period everyday to come out of their cells because of the nature of their war crimes.

We spent about five days covering this prison camp until another group from a different battalion came to take over our duties. At this time, we returned to Stuttgart to await further orders.

Beginning of the Journey Home from Europe:

My journey home began when I left Stuttgart, Germany. On the way to Lehavre, France, which was the port from where we would eventually leave for the United States, we stopped at a small town called Kirsch Bromback in Germany. Cavanaugh, Servant, Gregoire, and I stayed there for two days in a small house at the edge of a field where there was a carousel about 100 feet from the porch of the house. It was similar to what you would find in a traveling carnival in the United States. Its music (an organ that played most of the time) was a song called "You Can't Be True, Dear." To this day, this song is still embedded in my brain.

From Kirsch Brombach, we eventually wound up in Camp Chesterfield. We were fed well, and our papers were finalized to go to our next destination, Lehavre, France. We boarded a ship called "The Webster Victory." It was a small ship which accommodated about 500 of us. It was one of many ships called victory ships which were built on the west coast by a man named Kaiser and which had been turned out about one every other week during the war effort. My bunk was as low in the ship as you could get. On November 22nd, my birthday, we set sail into the Atlantic Ocean where, soon afterward, we were hit by a hurricane. By the sound of it, it seemed like the bottom of the ship would split in half. At one point, I wanted to go on deck to see the severity of the storm. As I tried to open a door to the deck, the wind and rain threw the door and me back. I stood there, realizing that had I gotten out, I would have been washed overboard.

We were blown far off course toward Bermuda. What should have been about a six day voyage took almost 14 days. Eventually, we docked, and we were sent to Fort Dix in New Jersey for further separation procedures. After a couple of days, those of us slated for total separation at Fort Devens were put on a train heading for Massachusetts. I experienced a weird feeling, as en route to our destination, the train went through Bridgeport, Connecticut, my hometown and initial point of departure three years earlier. From the train window, I could see the main district of Bridgeport with its theaters, restaurants, and most of all, the place where I worked at my first job.

Once at Devens, we went through another physical examination and were questioned as to whether or not we had anything wrong with us. Most of us were anxious to get home, so our answers were in the negative. I, personally, was experiencing severe headaches, but did not mention this and passed the physical.

As anxious as we were to get home, the three days at Devens were quite interesting. Devens was not far from Jimmy Cavanaugh's mother-in-law's house, and he, Chuck Resseguie, Clovis Servant, and I managed to get out of the camp by calling for a cab. As we went by the MP at the gate of the camp, we flashed a blank piece of paper, hoping he would not look at it, as it was not a pass, and it worked. From there, we stopped at a diner, and I ordered a piece of blueberry pie and a tall glass of cold milk. Wow! What a treat! Then, at Cavanaugh's mother-in-law's house, we were treated to more food and hospitality.

We managed to get back to Fort Devens that evening just in time to check in and hear "Taps." As I already mentioned, to this day, "Taps" still brings tears to my eyes.

The Parting of Friends and the Train Ride Home:

Jim Cavanaugh, Clovis Servant, and I left Fort Devens together. We had become very close during the war. When we got to Worcester, Massachusetts, we went into a bar and had a final drink together. Then, with strong hugs, we vowed to keep in touch and to see each other every five years, and we went our separate ways. Coming together again was taken care of by post war reunions. A group from our battalion created a 486th battalion organization which in its charter had a president and officers who would be responsible for bi-annual reunions in different cities in New England. Years later, the reunions took place annually, as we were losing members due to the inevitable process of life.

After boarding a train in Worcester, Massachusetts, I would later have to switch to a train in Springfield, Massachusetts in order to reach my hometown of Bridgeport, Connecticut. While on the train to Bridgeport, I sat opposite a lieutenant from another armored division who spotted my 3rd Armored patch and suggested that we have a drink. I agreed, although I still had not gotten over the drink I had downed in Worcester. We finished the officer's bottle of scotch, wished each other well, and soon the voice of the conductor came over the intercom system to say that we were coming into the Bridgeport station.

As I stepped off of the train, I was greeted by my brother, Morris, and my brother-in-law, Max. I was partially inebriated and "feeling my oats." Off we went to my parents' home, where my sisters Ethel and Rose, sister-in-law Irene, and my mother and father greeted me with open arms. They were overwhelmed with happiness. The first thing that my father said after recovering from the initial reunion moment was "Come, have a drink with me to celebrate your homecoming." Of course, I had it, in spite of the fact that I had already had my share of drinks, as it was one drink that I would never turn down. Mom made sure that she prepared my old bed for me for when it came time to retire. However, when morning came, she found me sleeping on the floor. I told her that I had to get used to sleeping again in such comfort. Incidentally, it took only one night to sleep in the bed at home once more.

Post Discharge:

I was discharged from the Army on December 10, 1945. Having become a "world traveler" during the war, I did not intend to stay at home but instead wanted to go to California. However, I put it "on the back burner" because I was influenced by thoughts of my aging parents needing me at home. They had been praying for my safety every night that I had been gone during the war and had both turned totally gray. I also was offered the opportunity of becoming a second lieutenant because of my combat record if I were to go back to the Army within 30 days. If I accepted the offer, the commission would be given to me in Paris, but I turned it down. In my mind, I felt that later I might go to California to see more of the United States.

How I Met My Wife:

It was February of 1946 when fate, in which I am a strong believer, stepped in. I received a telephone call from a girl who was the sister of a fellow in my battalion in the Army. She worked with another girl who would eventually become my wife. The telephone call was in regard to an invitation to a party which was to take place on the following Saturday night. The girl called me because her brother had told her about me and said that I would be a nice guy to invite to a party. I already had plans for that night to go on a date with a girl in Waterbury, Connecticut, and as funny as it may seem, the buffalo on the back of a nickel determined what I would choose to do and my future.

Saturday night was a blistery cold night, and I was having second thoughts about whether or not to go to Waterbury because of the bad weather. I took a nickel from my pocket, tossed it in the air, and said to myself "If the Indian comes up, I will go to Waterbury. If the buffalo comes up, I will go to the party." The buffalo came up, I went to the party, and I ended up meeting the woman who would eventually be my wife.

Upon arriving at the party, I noticed an attractive young lady with jet black hair and flashing brown eyes serving refreshments. I asked a Marine who was standing alongside of me whether he knew her, and he said that he did not. I responded by saying "I would like to marry a girl like her." In the past, most of the girls I had dated were Italian, and this girl looked Italian too. When she approached me to offer me some refreshments, there was an instant chemistry between us, and I actually felt jealous when she danced with other guys.

I had the opportunity to leave the party with her, as someone who had a car suggested that we go with him and his date to Seaside Park where there was a hot dog stand. Can you believe that a hot dog with bacon, mustard, and relish was only 10 cents? When I brought the young woman home later that evening, I saw that the name plate on the door was "Levine." I realized then that she was not Italian, but Jewish. I knew that my feelings for her were genuine, as I offered to stoke her parents' furnace that evening.

Molly and I were engaged within six months and exchanged wedding vows on November 24, 1945. Now, in the year 2010, we will have been married 64 years. I am thankful that I had a nickel in my pocket and that as fate would have it, the buffalo head turned up on the flip of the coin that Saturday night in 1945. As the result of our marriage, we were blessed with three children, Deborah, Mindy, and Michael (who unexpectedly tragically died and left us at the young age of 20) and wonderful grandchildren, Benjamin, Jenna, and Michael.

Additional Individual War Experiences
Somewhere in Belgium:

My track was in a position near one of our M-16s, which in turn was positioned near a small house situated on top of a slight hill. Now try to picture this:

In this house lived a Belgian policeman, or Gendarme, with a lovely wife and an equally attractive daughter. Each morning of the week that we spent in this area, at exactly 8 a.m., the policeman would leave his home and jauntily bounce down the steps, looking sharp in his uniform. He would get on his bicycle, and away he would ride down the hill. Within minutes of his departure, the M-16 crew would go into the house and have coffee with his wife and daughter. My driver Greg and I would stand guard while the crew was inside the house, and we would watch for enemy aircraft. Among the crew of the M-16, three were from Maine and of French descent, so consequently, they were able to speak fluent French and converse freely with the women. The men would not stay in the house very long, knowing that a full crew was needed to operate their M-16.

This scenario went on for a week. The Gendarme went off in the morning and came home at night at the same time, and I believe he was never aware of the morning "coffee sessions." (If he was suspicious of anything, he probably would have chosen to stay home and have coffee with them.) However, the M-

16 crew swore to Greg and me that the meetings were strictly coffee and conversation. (Enough said.)

* * * * * *

My track, with a full complement of five men in it, had to go back into Belgium for a minor repair. It was toward evening when we ran across what appeared to be a Red Cross building. We stopped, as we were hungry and had seen people coming out of the building with coffee and doughnuts. We were dirty and tired and did not wish to go in, so I told my buddies that I would go into the building to get the coffee and snacks and bring it to them. The people who were dishing out the food said that my buddies would have to come inside to have it. I watched as civilians were being allowed to take things out of the building, yet we, the soldiers who had fought for and liberated their country, were told that we had to come in to be served. I was very angry and told them off in no uncertain terms with some explicit adjectives. Although I was so angry that I felt I could have leveled the place with my machine gun, my conscience told me otherwise. Reasoning with myself, I realized that these were not Americans running the place, but Belgian citizens who were following orders and also favoring their friends. Having been liberated by us, though, I felt that they should have made an exception to their normal protocol and used some common sense. I suppose that if I had insisted on taking out the food, I could have done so, but instead, we moved on and discovered an English group of soldiers who were billeted a short way down the road. They cheerfully greeted us and told us we were welcome to stay to eat with them at their evening meal. I recall that it consisted of a fish dinner. Then they also gave us cots and blankets, and we stayed with them for the night. In the morning, we thanked them and went on our way. I feel that this is the way we should have been treated by the Belgians at the Red Cross building.

* * * * * *

One of my pleasant memories was coming into the town of Liege. People were milling around and thanking us for the liberation of their city. We pulled up into a square outside of a creamery. What a treat! A short while later, as we moved through the town, we came to a stop, and it appeared that we would be there for awhile. Leaving our track in the hands of our radio maintenance man, Greg and I went into a bar. Behind the bar, there were four men and two women. One of the women took us into the back room. She left and then came back with bowls of hot soup for Greg and me. There was a record player nearby, and she put on a record and danced with each of us for about a minute. She told us that the five of them were part of the underground. Worrying about whether or not our track was moving, we thanked her and left. When we exited the building, the other woman who had been behind the bar was standing inside of a doorway across the road holding a rifle. As I walked up to her to talk to her, she abruptly left. I assume that if she had talked to me, it could have been dangerous for her.

When we left this establishment, our track was still in the same spot. We walked up the street, and there, in front of a restaurant, stood a lady with her arms crossed. She spoke perfect English and invited us in. Compared to the place that we had just left, this was a palace. There were glass mirrors all around and very fancy tables and chairs. We stood at the bar, and she mixed us what I thought were martinis because of the effect the drinks had on us. Then she invited us upstairs into an apartment. Seeing how dirty we were, she gave us basins of water from which we could wash our face and hands and her husband's shaving equipment so that we could shave. After cleaning up, she cooked eggs for us. She told us that she had been born in New

York City and after World War I had met her Belgian husband who had been a soldier. As she was more than middle aged, her husband must have been the same. She could not account for his present whereabouts.

After we had eaten, we looked out the window and noticed that our track was still down the street and that there had been no movement. We felt we had pressed our luck too far, so we wanted to leave in a hurry. We thanked her and hastened out of the door.

Somewhere in France:

Going through an area of a small town in our half-track, on one of the corners, I noticed four people lying on a sidewalk. I assumed they were a family, as there were two adults and two children. There were no signs of life around, and the area itself seemed to be deserted, except for the four people who looked as if they might be dead. We were moving rather slowly, but could not stop, as we were involved in a combat situation. I felt that these people must have been hit by fragments of a shell or some sort of gunfire. As we passed them, I hoped that they were not dead, that perhaps they still had some life left in them, and that someone would come to their assistance.

* * * * * *

This particular short story is one that tears at your heart. Our track was in convoy and slowly moving through a town. I heard screaming and all kinds of shouting. Operating my radio under a canvas cover, I moved up front to where my driver sat to see what it was all about. What I saw was a young lady being literally dragged up the road by her hair by several men and women. Her screaming mother was trying to hold her back. It was all about the girl having been labeled as a collaborator with the Germans, and this was her punishment. While they were dragging her, one of the women had a scissor and was cutting off her hair. It was extremely hard to watch. At a later time, I had the opportunity to ask another French girl at a bar whether she had ever fraternized with the Germans. She said that she had, but that this was the only way she could buy food and clothing, as she did not know the whereabouts of her husband who had been taken away by the Germans.

* * * * * *

In the town of Gavray, we had settled into a position for the evening. In our area as well as others, there were single planes that would appear and wreak some havoc every evening. GIs had their own names for these planes, and we called ours "Bed Check Charlie." One could tell "Bed Check Charlie" was not one of our planes by the drone of his engine. One night before I had closed my radio station transmissions, I heard him overhead. One of our M15s was nearby, and I radioed his call letters and said to him, "What do you say? Let's try to bring him down!" Although it was nighttime and pitch dark, and I should not have had him open fire, we went ahead and did it. It was the last time "Bed Check Charlie" would fly over us, as he was brought down. I experienced no repercussions over it, and the next morning, a picture was taken of the plane and the pilot lying alongside of it, minus his brain.

* * * * * *

Apparently the division had captured a food warehouse which had dozens and dozens of fresh eggs. Captain DeFranco came up to our track and told us that we had received some eggs that the division had disbursed to different units. Our track's portion of the disbursement proved to be close to 20 dozen eggs. We had not had fresh eggs in a long time, and we were anxious to get at them. There were five of us in the crew, and we went to work making scrambled, hard boiled, and whatever type of eggs we could make. Believe it or not, within 30 hours, those eggs were just about gone. As each of us had eaten way too many eggs in such a short period of time, we paid for our gluttony shortly afterward by being constipated for a few days. As anxious as we had been to eat those eggs when we first got them, at this point, we did not care whether we ever saw an egg again!

* * * * * *

One time I decided to check out a wooded area. Upon doing so, I saw in the distance a tall, red headed German soldier, with his back toward me, and one foot on a shovel, apparently in the process of digging. I approached him as quietly and stealthily as I could so that he would not hear me and perhaps turn around violently. I put my M1 in his back, ready to pull the trigger if necessary. As I pressed it against him, he toppled forward. To my surprise, the man was dead. He must have been shot and killed much earlier, and rigor mortis had set in. Even though he was dead, his body was in an upright position when I discovered him because his hands were still holding the shovel which was planted firmly in the ground.

Upon checking his uniform, I noticed his gas canister had the same numbers - 486 - as my own battalion numbers. I removed it from him with the intention of keeping it as a souvenir. Somewhere along the way, however, someone took it from my track, and I did not question anyone about it.

Somewhere in Germany:

How it came about, I do not recall, but there I was, sitting on a rock alongside of a dirt road, and several feet from me, also sitting on a rock, was General Hickey. We were both having lunch which consisted of K-rations. We did not engage in any conversation, but as we sat there, a 2 ½ ton army truck passed by us. It was loaded with bodies of GIs who had paid the ultimate price. General Hickey and I looked at each other. At this moment, the picture was one of two men with different ranks (one, a sergeant, and the other, a general) who both shared the same feeling - an extremely sad one.

* * * * * *

Once in awhile, we would become stalemated in an area. Gregoire, Barlow, and I would leave our track in order to stretch out on the ground close enough to the track so that I could still hear my radios. One time, as I was stretched out on the ground, I looked to my left, and there was a bent leg protruding out of the ground from the knee to the toes. Apparently, the leg belonged to a German soldier, as the trouser was part of a German uniform. His friends must have buried him in a hurry. In addition, what was even more surprising and disturbing was that not only was his leg protruding, but I actually saw his eyeballs and fingernails on the ground. Weird!

* * * * * *

We pulled up to a German farmhouse, and I decided to enter it to see whether it was inhabited. Inside, there was a family who was sitting down at a table eating a meal. There were three girls sitting with their parents, and when they took one look at me, they let out shrieks and ran down into the cellar. At that moment, I could not understand how I could strike such fear into somebody. Upon further thought, I realized that my face was very dirty and unshaven and that I was also carrying an M1 and a shoulder pistol; I didn't look like the kind of person one would want to befriend. I spoke to the adults and told them that I was just looking for German soldiers and that nobody would be harmed. The parents of the girls reassured them that no one was going to be hurt, so they came out of the cellar, and I left.

* * * * * *

It is amazing how one can see small bits of horrible things, and although they affect you for the moment, you go on and "forget" them a short while later. I do not mean to say that they are totally forgotten, as they are permanently etched in your mind. I am just trying to say that they do not consciously and intensely affect you on a day to day basis throughout your life. Of the hundreds of horrors I came across, one was of a German soldier who lay on the ground. His body was intact, but his head was crushed as flat as a pancake, and his profile was still evident. I took his wallet out of his pants pocket to look for some identification. In it was a picture of his wife and children. At this point, I did not look further for identification, for even though he was the enemy, I had some feeling for him and those he left behind.

* * * * * *

Not too far from the area where I had discovered the body of the soldier with a flattened head, there four German soldiers sitting in a burning vehicle - two in front and two in back. They must have been hit by a shell. To me, they looked like four burning candles, as their heads and bodies were aflame.

* * * * * *

There was one time when Greg and I and our track were situated for communication purposes quite far away from Battery C vehicles. At a certain point, we had to rejoin the main part of the Battery; however, we became lost. We took a right turn where we should have gone straight. As we came down a stretch of hill, there was a small town a distance away. All of a sudden, we saw a few planes behind some of the buildings going into the air. We realized why at that moment. The German town was in the process of being taken, and behind us, at the top of the hill and coming down the hill, were five U.S. tanks firing shells over our heads into the town. Apparently, we were very close to our own group, as Captain De-Franco and his driver Anctil came down the road, pulled alongside of us, and directed us to where we should have gone.

* * * * * *

My half-track and some elements of C Battery came to a halt in a small town (I believe the town was Eilendorf). On one side of the road were about six small houses. Being that I was a sergeant and the highest ranking non com in the group, the only lieutenant that we had with us came over to me and gave me a direct order. He phrased it this way: "As we haven't slept in beds for a long time, Sergeant, I want you to evacuate those houses, and tonight we will." Of course, I had to do as I was told (although I did not want to). The first five houses were a cinch. They were inhabited by young couples who understood why I gave them these orders. However, when it came to the last house, the door was opened by an elderly lady who reminded me of my mother. I looked over her shoulder, and in a dimly lit and poorly furnished room, I saw a young woman holding a baby. On the floor was a straw basket, which obviously was where the baby slept. Although the older woman did not know yet what I was about to say and the reason for my being there, she fell to her knees and began to plead with me not to harm them. I reached down, and with both hands under her elbows, I lifted her to her feet and told her that no one would harm them; although I had been ordered to evacuate the houses, she and the young lady and the baby would stay in the house. She told me that the young woman was her daughter and that the baby was her grandchild. The girl's husband was in the German army, and she did not know whether he was alive or dead. Reassuring their safety, I left that last house. The lieutenant confronted me as I left and asked me whether the mission had been accomplished. He was angry when I told him that the last house was staying. I was angrier than him, as I talked back to him in a tone not becoming of a sergeant talking to a superior. I was disturbed in part because I felt that after sleeping in the elements for the duration of the war, we could have gone on as we had without throwing people out of their homes. Consequently, however, the whole incident was for naught, as a march order was issued, and we left the area. Little did we know that we soon would face a grave situation on the outskirts of Dessau.

* * * * * *

With our half-track nearby, Greg and I had laid down in a field to try to relax. Out of nowhere, a German plane zoomed down and strafed us. Thank God, the bullets missed us, but not by much! It was unusual that it did not try to hit our half-track and did not make a second pass but instead just took off; maybe the pilot had no more ammunition.

* * * * * *

In Germany, I watched a P-38 and an aerial dog fight in which the P-38 was split in half and the jet disappeared out of sight with unbelievable speed. I believe that it was one of the first jets used in the war.

* * * * * *

During our occupation, members of the 486th were invited to a barbecue at a German castle. Also invited were women of the WRENS English army so that we would have the company of the opposite sex. Needless to say, situations arose, and we were never invited anywhere again.

* * * * * *

One morning in the town of Wixhausen, while waiting to be sent home, a lieutenant, who had been a very good friend of mine through combat, told me something which should have made me angry. Instead, I shrugged it off. I had been selected by a group of officers to receive a bronze star for meritorious service as a communication sergeant because I never left my radio under fire or any other life threatening circumstances, which could have put others' lives at stake. This lieutenant apologized for entering another soldier's name to receive the bronze star. He explained that he chose this man because the man was not well, and he felt that it would get the man home earlier. Of course, if I had received the bronze star, I could have gotten home earlier too, but I tried to be understanding. At the time, because our meeting was spontaneous, the importance of what he told me didn't register fully, and I readily accepted his apology. What remains important to me is that in my battalion book, my battery commander wrote the words "Swirsky, a job well done." In my mind, that took the place of any medals or commendations I could have received.

* * * * * *

In the town of Gressenich, at 2 o'clock in the morning, Gregoire and I received an order to immediately come to a small tent which housed two lieutenants. The "emergency" was that they wanted us to play 4-handed pinochle with them. They treated us like their equals while we ate popcorn and played cards. To say the least, this was a very unusual situation. I don't think that it would have been acceptable by army standards.

Memories

Celebrities Who Performed for Us:

Marlene Dietrich performed in Normandy, France. With artillery sounds in the background, she sang the song "Lilly Marlene" for us in a barn with a makeshift platform. After she sang, three GIs were allowed to go up to her, and she hugged and kissed each of them. They returned to their places "on cloud nine."

Jack Benny also visited us and was accompanied by a singer named Martha Tilton. Additionally, we had the pleasure of seeing Ingrid Bergman in the city of Darmstadt after the war. She signed many autographs for the soldiers.

Another celebrity who visited the 3rd Armored Division was Bob Hope. He was accompanied by Billy Conn, the prize fighter, and also by "Parkurcarcus," a comedian, and Jerry Colonna, also a comedian. Lilly Pons also sang in a Cologne auditorium center.

Songs We Sang:

In the States, we heard on the juke boxes continuously "The Red Rose of Texas," "I'll be With you in Apple Blossom Time," "Don't Fence Me In," "White Christmas," "I'm Gonna Buy Myself a Paper Doll," "The Bells are Ringing for Me and

My Gall," "When the Lights Go on Again All Over the World," and "White Cliffs of Dover." In England, for the most part, we heard "Roll Me Over in the Clover," "It's a Long Way to Tipperary," "Yankee Doodle Dandy," "Over There, Over There, It Won't Be Over 'Til We Are Over There," "The Hokey Pokey," and "Lilly Marlene."

Post War Experiences:

If I was walking down the street and a car backfired, I would automatically interpret the sound as a gunshot and look for my M1 rifle. At first, I would feel ridiculous, but then I would realize that it was a post war reaction.

If I went to a carnival, I would avoid walking in front of a shooting gallery, even though I knew the guns were chained.

One time, my wife and I attended a Broadway play. On the stage, one of the actors abruptly pulled out a gun and shot another actor. It was so sudden that it left me in a cold sweat. I often thought that if I had a gun on me at the time, I would have fired it at the actor on stage.

Throughout the time that I was experiencing a lot of these post war incidents, my brother-in-law, Wolf, who had been part of a medical unit in St. Lo during the war in Europe, suggested that I see a doctor who had been his commanding officer. My wife and I traveled to see this doctor in New York. After a thorough examination, he told me that there was absolutely nothing physically wrong with me. His actual remarks were "Your wife is pregnant. You are a healthy man. Get the heck out of here, and learn to live with yourself!" On the way home, we stopped at my sister-in-law's home. Something happened next that seemed uncanny, but that seemed to be very fitting. As I sat at her kitchen table, I glanced at a calendar on the wall with the pages of each month bearing a wise quote from a a prominent person. The statement that I happened to read was one expressed by President Franklin D. Roosevelt. It read "We have nothing to fear but fear itself." That saying immediately reinforced what the doctor had just told me and also affected me in a positive way. It is something I have always gone back to for reassurance.

A Recurring Dream:

The uneasiness I felt in combat stayed with me as I re-entered civilian life and affected my ability to get any consistent sleep. Back home, I grew to hate the long, dark fall and winter nights, as they reminded me of the ones I experienced in combat where I did not know what was going on around me. I shared with my wife that if I only could hear the firing of a machine gun or other weapons of war, as opposed to the stillness of the night, I could probably better relax. In other words, the quietness of my own bedroom at home was more unsettling to me than all of the noises of war to which I had become accustomed. Additionally, in the war, because of the type of duty I had to perform (the operation of three radios, one of which was Morse Code), I slept about two or three hours only during a 24 hour period, and sleep took the form of cat naps.

By the time I met my wife Molly, flashbacks and nightmares that I had been having since returning home from the war had begun to intensify. She was the recipient of a husband who was not only having a nightmare each night, but was experiencing the same recurrent one night after night.

Each night, upon falling asleep, I dreamt that I was chasing a black charred figure. Whenever I got close to it, I could not grasp it. At this point in the dream, I would groan and toss the sheets and wake up my wife who would quiet me down. My body would be cold, and I would be shivering. One evening, the situation was so bad that she called our family doctor at 1 a.m. As doctors made house calls in those days, he came to the house and gave me a sedative to quiet me down. Before he left, I heard him talking to my wife about the fact that I was probably on the edge of a nervous breakdown. This was not meant for me to hear, and I was greatly disturbed having read in the newspapers stories about discharged veterans and what they were doing to themselves due to their traumatized states of mind.

The dream finally ceased to occur when one night, while in the middle of the dream and as I was chasing the figure, it stopped abruptly and turned around so that it was facing me. Instead of continuing to try to grasp the figure, I stopped dead in my tracks. Then the figure started to rise. As it did, only its face began to become clear and recognizable to me. It was the face of a neighbor who I remember had been a soft spoken and gentle man when I was about 10 years old. His face was as smooth as a porcelain doll's, and he smiled at me. With this smile, the entire figure faded away, and I have never since had that dream. Much later in life, I met this man's son and told him of the recurring dream I had about his dad for several years. He analyzed it by saying that his dad must have been my guardian angel.

Accomplishments of the
486th AAA (AW) (SP) Battalion:

I am proud to have been a part of the 486th AAA AW (SP) battalion and to have shared in its many accomplishments and succeses. Men of the 486th constantly demonstrated their versatility with 50 caliber quadruple mounts and 37 mm automatic cannons. Whether the target was enemy aircraft or German tanks, Colonel Dunnington's anti-aircraft soldiers were ready and willing to engage them in the air and on the ground. It was confirmed that we damaged and destroyed everything from light bombing planes to jet-propelled fighters. On ground targets, documented figures show that the battalion destroyed more than 225 German combat vehicles including tanks, armored cars, horse drawn artillery pieces, and a minimum of two railway trains. The battalion was the first of its kind on German soil in World War II and also the first to shoot down an enemy aircraft on German soil (accomplished by Russell Eicke of C Battery). In addition, the 486th ack-ack group expended as much ammunition on ground forces as they had on enemy aircraft.

Some of the Division "Firsts":

First to cross the Belgian border.
First to fire a shell into Germany.
First to cross the German border in the area of Eupen.
First to capture a German town.
First to breach the Siegfried Line.
First to shoot down an enemy plane on German soil.
First to capture a major city - Cologne.
First to accomplish the greatest one-day advance in the history of mobile warfare - 101 miles.

In addition, I would like to give credit to some of the many divisions who did their share in winning World War II, such as the 82nd Airborne, the Big Red One Infantry, and the 101st Airborne. Also, one must not forget the P-47 Thunderbolts, who, at the crack of dawn, when they were not hampered by cloud cover, would strafe the enemy from morning to dusk. They were instrumental in clearing the way for our advancing. Then there were the infantry soldiers who, in my estimation, were the backbone of any ensuing conflict, and who exhibited enormous bravery in spite of having to take tremendous losses, along with the medics, who put their lives on the line every minute of the day and night to help the wounded. In addition, we should remember the Piper Cubs, small planes who spotted the enemy for us, and the MPs (military police) who directed our vehicles at important locations. I also recall the Red Ball Express trucks which, around the clock, carried supplies, gasoline, and whatever was needed to conduct the war to the troops upfront.

Finally, I would be remiss if I did not mention the men and women who did not participate in combat but who were so vital in planning and plotting the strategy of the war and also the army nurses and doctors who compassionately cared for the injured.

General Rose of the 3rd Armored Division:

It seems that every time I speak of the 3rd Armored Division to someone, they immediately say "Oh, you were with General Patton," and I respond "No, General Rose" (who incidentally was one of the most unheralded great generals of World War II). It seems that General Patton was in the 2nd Armored Division, Third Army, and General Rose was in the 3rd Armored Division, First Army. Consequently, when the press would write about the 3rd Armored Division's accomplishments, because of the similarity in the words, the credits were often attributed to General Patton's 3rd Army, and not the 3rd Armored, as they should have been. Not only did General Rose serve in Europe at the head of the 3rd Armored Division (which he felt was the greatest tank force in the world and one worthy of the title "Spearhead"), but he also served with the 1st armored divisions ("Old Ironsides") in Africa and Italy and the second armored division ("Hell on Wheels"). I was so proud to have served under General Rose, as he believed that he belonged at the head of his troops in battle, not somewhere behind the lines, mapping out the strategy while his men did the fighting. Because of his bravery in always spearheading his troops, he died heroically at the head of a column.

Epilogue:

Whenever I have spoken of my participation in World War II, many people have asked me whether I have ever gone back to the cities and battlefields where I had fought in France, Belgium, and Germany. In September of 1994, 84 people, including my wife Molly and I , Third Armored "Spearheaders," and a few children and grandchildren, went back to Europe and on two buses toured the 21 major cities that we had liberated in 21 days. The tour was arranged two years previously by a committee of our 3rd Armored Division and a committee of people from France and Belgium, Of course, as Germany had been the enemy, we communicated with only one city in that country – Stolberg. Only the mayor of Stolberg contacted us and invited us to his city, as no one else was made aware of our visit, and he arranged a special meeting for a certain date and time. We came into Stolberg very "quietly," stopped in front of the Town Hall, entered the building, and sat at a long table where we were served drinks and snacks. I sat next to a German soldier who had one arm missing as the result of fighting in the war. He shook my hand with his good arm, and it was amazing how after being enemies in World War II, we could now amiably acknowledge each other. The mayor spoke through an interpreter and thanked us because of the fact that during the war, before our soldiers entered the city, the citizens had been told to expect us to rape their women and take their food, and instead, we did just the opposite. We respected their citizens and gave them food. The mayor also thanked us for liberating them from Hitler.

Other highlights of the trip included the following:

In France, being on Omaha Beach again brought back vivid memories. Molly and I went down into a German bunker which gave us an uncanny feeling to realize that German guns had been shooting from this bunker at the invading Allied Forces. As we traveled through the cities of this country, people lined the street curbs, shouting and waving. In some of the cities where we stopped, if it was close to lunchtime, we were given meals and/or refreshments. Also in France, we visited the American cemeteries, which were immaculately kept. At one cemetery, two of our 486th Battalion men were buried.

In Belgium, the reception we were given was fantastic! Children were given the day off from school so that they and their teachers could be a part of the celebration. They lined the streets, waving American flags and shouting greetings. We threw the children packets of Third Armored pins (which also included sticks of gum). There were marching bands too, which made the visit quite exhilarating. The main highlight, though, was returning to Bastogne, the location of the Battle of the Bulge, where I received a medal for participation in this crucial battle.

In Germany, the most "moving" stop was at the site of the Nordhausen concentration camp. The silence there was so eery that one could hear a pin drop. Although it was not one of the more pleasant parts of our tour and the memories it brought to mind were somewhat disturbing/upsetting, as this was a place where such horrific atrocities occurred, it was an important and necessary place to see on our trip. In Germany, we also visited the West Wall, which was the partition between East and West Germany, and we viewed two of Berlin's most historical landmarks, the Reichstag, which is the seat of the German Parliament, and the Brandenburger Gate. Then it was on to Berlin and back home to the good old U.S.A.

Acknowledgments to:

My wonderful wife of 64 years, Molly, for her unwavering support and encouragement in the writing of my book and for always finding a way to push me back on track when I faltered.

My daughter, Mindy Hart, who put in endless hours on the computer, and without whom I could not have put together my book.

My daughter and son-in-law, Doctors Deborah Swirsky-Sacchetti and Thomas Swirsky-Sacchetti, for their invaluable help in getting My War into print and for their steadfast support.

My grandson, Michael Hart, a very talented 12 year old, who made suggestions about and helped in designing both front and back covers, and my grandson's friend, Peter Keefe, who supported Mike's ideas.

My grandson, Benjamin Sacchetti, and my granddaughter, Jenna Swirsky-Sacchetti, for their enthusiastic support and willingness to listen with respect and pride to my war stories over the years.

Elaine Frazer, a family friend, who was responsible for my decision to write My War. Her husband Bill was a Navy Veteran in World War II.

Carol Gursky and Dick Goodie, two accomplished writers who have published books, for their valuable advice.

Curt Giles and Dom Rizzo, two army buddies, who supplied pictures and addresses of former comrades.

Tom Holzack, for reading the beginning of my book and offering further help if needed.

Vic Damon, for his advice and contributions to my book, including pictures of Colonel Dunnington, General Bradley, and General Rose.

Glenn Gundersen, for his legal counsel.

Nayan, James, and Sean, of The UPS Store of Milford, Connecticut, who willingly helped and showed patience in reproducing my pictures.

And last, but not least, all my family and friends who have cared to listen and encouraged me to share my story.